HABIT DE POLICHINEL NAPOLITAIN

HABIT DE SCARAMOUCHE NAPOLITAIN

HABIT D'ARLEQUIN MODERNE

HABIT D'ARLEQUIN ANCIEN

Illustration from Luigi Riccoboni's
Histoire du Théâtre Italienne,
published 1728

The Victoria and Albert Museum, London (Crown Copyright)

Scent Bottles

A CONNOISSEUR MONOGRAPH

General Editor: Frank Davis

Scent Bottles

Kate Foster

THE CONNOISSEUR

and MICHAEL JOSEPH

London 1966

Designed and produced for The Connoisseur,
Chestergate House, Vauxhall Bridge Road, London SW1,
and Michael Joseph Ltd, 26 Bloomsbury Street, London WC1
by George Rainbird Ltd, 2 Hyde Park Place, London W2
Filmset in Linofilm by Graphic Film Limited Dublin Ireland
and printed and bound by Kultura, Budapest, Hungary.
House Editor: Mary Anne Norbury
Typographer: Nan Quelle

First published 1966

PRINTED IN HUNGARY

Contents

Acknowledgements

WHILE gathering material for this book I have been fortunate enough to have access to several fine collections of scent bottles. Foremost among these is the Houbigant Collection in Paris, and I should especially like to thank M. Fernand Javal for his kindness in allowing me to examine and photograph his fine collection. I should also like to thank Mrs Derek Fitzgerald for allowing me to illustrate bottles from the collection of the late Mrs Meyer Sassoon, and Mrs Claude Leigh and Sir Hugh Dawson for their help and for permitting me to illustrate some of their bottles; and the museums mentioned in the captions and Sotheby & Co. for permission to use photographs. Many members of the English Ceramic Circle were kind enough to send me information and photographs of bottles, and, while I have been unable to illustrate most of these, I am extremely grateful for their help. I particularly wish to thank Mr Robert Williams for his help and comments in the grouping of Chelsea bottles, and Mr and Mrs Frank Tilley for their encouragement. Many of the French perfume houses helped me in my researches, and my thanks are especially due to the houses of Guerlain, Lancôme, and Lanvin. My family and friends have given me help and moral support, but I am particularly indebted to Miss Cecilia Gray for her photographic work, and to Mr John Cornforth for his patience and hard work in going through my manuscript.

K.F

List of Colour Plates

List of Illustrations

1 Speaking Generally

Who that has reason, and his smell,
Would not among roses and jasmine dwell,
Rather than all his spirits choke
With exhalations of dirt and smoke?
—Cowley, *Of Gardens*

FOR CENTURIES the art of perfumery has occupied the minds of craftsmen, scientists, and dilettantes. Much thought has gone into its invention and the development of different kinds from a profusion of flowers and herbs, into the use of them, and into the design of containers for such sweet and precious scents. Every material that can be imagined has at one time or another been employed for scent bottles, and, depending on the fashion of the day, one or another has been particularly favoured.

For the first contribution to perfumery, one has to turn back approximately three thousand years, to the Eighteenth Dynasty in Egypt. Then, lavish use of perfumes and aromatic herbs was made in religious ceremonies, particularly in connection with the elaborate formulas for embalming the dead, when myrrh, cinnamon, and other rich spices were used. Evidence of this tradition can be seen in tombs in Egypt, where scent bottles have been found among the treasure, and where wall-paintings depict them in scenes of everyday life. Naturally embalmment was restricted to the wealthy, who alone could afford the luxury of such a burial. Heavy incense and perfumes were also used in religious processions. At banquets, guests would be anointed with perfume and garlanded with sweet-smelling flowers, including the lotus and the crocus, before being permitted to take their places at the table.

Perfume vessels at this time were chiefly of glass. These were made by winding opaque glass in a molten state around a core of sand. They came chiefly from the Nile Delta and from along the Phoenician coast. Strict security surrounded their places of manufacture, and in Alexandria, the chief centre of the trade, each workman before leaving at the end of a day was searched to avoid a leakage of the secret methods.

The fashion for scent and its containers spread and flourished further afield. In Greece, perfume became such an obsession that, instead of meeting in the local café or its contemporary equivalent, fashionable Greeks met their friends in perfume shops. Socrates and Solon proclaimed against the custom, but all warnings went unheeded. In fact, perfume had more than mere vanity value, for it combatted all kinds of disease; Hyppocrita is said to have saved Athens from the plague by burning aromatic woods and hanging garlands of flowers in the streets. Vessels for perfume were made of terracotta as well as glass, and they took various forms, including the sandalled foot, human heads, and birds.

The Romans found great enjoyment and satisfaction in the use of herbs as an aphrodisiac, and men, as well as women, began to realize the influence that perfumes could have in the art of seduction. In Shakespeare's account of Cleopatra's victory over Antony, Enobarbus describes the scene of their first meeting, and how

> The barge she sat in, like a burnish'd throne,
> Burn'd on the water; the poop was beaten gold;
> Purple the sails, and so perfumed that
> The winds were love-sick with them . . . From the barge
> A strange invisible perfume hits the sense
> Of the adjacent wharfs.
>
> —*Antony and Cleopatra,* Act II, Sc. ii

Herbs were still used for burial, and it is said that Nero used more aromatic herbs for Poppaea's funeral than Arabia could have produced in ten years.

Though the art of perfumery waned to a certain extent with the arrival of Christianity, there is evidence that a great many spices were highly prized. For instance, when the three kings came to worship the infant Christ, they brought, as the most precious offerings, frankincense and myrrh (both gum resins) as well as gold.

Western Europeans were introduced to the use of spices and perfumes before the Roman Empire by the Carthaginian and Phoenician traders, who were then the great seafarers. This trade was revived a thousand years later by the Crusaders, who returned bearing tales of curious Eastern customs. Marco Polo must have been the bearer of many such tempting stories — enough to make any adventurous traveller set forth without delay to Constantinople and other rich eastern cities.

The first mention in France of the manufacture of perfume appears in the twelfth century, when Philippe-Auguste passed a statute forming the first guild of *parfumeurs*. When Catherine de' Medici arrived in France four hundred years later, she was accompanied by her private scent-maker, René le Florentin, who later set up his shop on the Pont du Change, supplying quantities of rare scents and also attracting a slightly different clientèle by selling a variety of poisons.

During the sixteenth to eighteenth centuries, the general interest in perfume was so great that it became one of the leading trades, giving great scope to an alliance between the perfume-makers and the jewellers and goldsmiths, who were so well equipped to provide splendidly mounted scent bottles. Craftsmen obtained the entrée into the households of every fashionable family in the land. During the reign of Louis XIV, the fashion gathered momentum until the court of Louis XV became known as "la Cour parfumée". A different scent was worn every day, and each one, it can be presumed, was contained in a beautiful bottle of its own. Perfume was also sprayed on ornamental objects; porcelain flowers mounted on ormolu stalks were given the appropriate scent, and wigs, gloves, and clothes were sprayed, not only to allure the opposite sex but to make up for infrequent washing. Madame de Pompadour is said to have spent as much as 500,000 francs a year on perfume alone, quite apart from the amount she must have spent on bottles. She apparently had great confidence in the perfume chosen for her by Lazare Duvaux, a jeweller and general trader, for he records her purchasing large amounts of "eau du Portugal" and "huile de Venus" and other perfumes.

During this period, innumerable bottles were made all over Europe, in porcelain, enamel, glass, gold, and silver, and in combinations of these materials. Undoubtedly the eighteenth century was the most fruitful period in the history of the scent bottle, and to this period can be traced many names that are still famous today. In 1774 there appeared in Paris a *parfumerie* called "A la

13

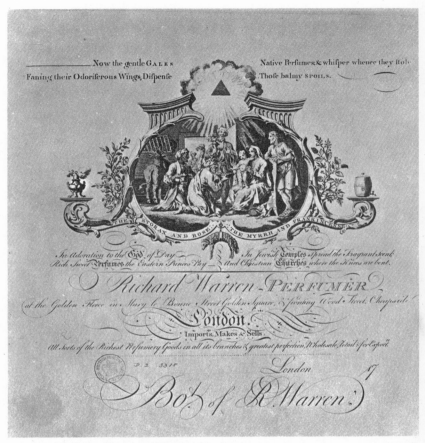

PLATE 1. Trade card, Richard Warren, Perfumer
The British Museum, London

Reine des Fleurs", and in 1775 the well-known name of Houbigant is mentioned for the first time. The family firm of Guerlain was founded in 1828, and it quickly became the official scent-manufacturer to the court of Napoleon III: one reminder of their early trade is a label on a bottle, still in their possession, that is inscribed "Eau aromatique de Montpellier, surnommée Eau des Souverains, pour la toilette, Guerlain No. 15, Rue de la Paix, Paris 1830". This particular *eau de toilette* was created specially for the beautiful Empress Eugénie.

In the nineteenth century, when the crafts associated with scent bottles started to go into decline, people began to collect old ones.

14

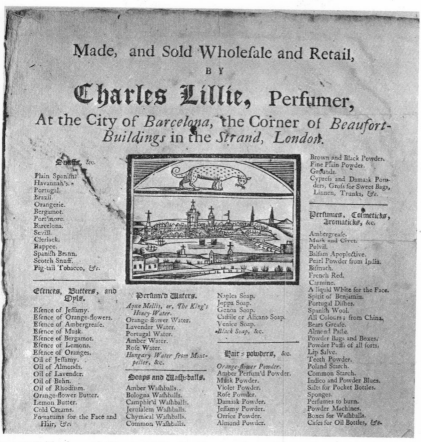

Made, and Sold Wholesale and Retail,

BY

Charles Lillie, Perfumer,

At the City of *Barcelona*, the Corner of *Beaufort-Buildings* in the *Strand*, *London*.

Snuff, &c.

Plain Spanish
Havannah's.
Portugal.
Brazil.
Orangerie.
Bergamot.
Port'more.
Barcelona.
Sevill.
Cleriack.
Rappee.
Spanish Bran.
Scotch Snuff.
Pig-tail Tobacco, &c.

Essences, Butters, and Oyls.

Essence of Jessamy.
Essence of Orange-flowers.
Essence of Ambergrease.
Essence of Musk.
Essence of Bergamot.
Essence of Lemons.
Essence of Oranges.
Oil of Jessamy.
Oil of Almonds.
Oil of Lavender.
Oil of Behn.
Oil of Rhodium.
Orange-flower Butter.
Lemon Butter.
Cold Creams.
Pomatums for the Face and Hair, &c.

Perfum'd Waters.

Aqua Mellis, or, The King's Honey-Water.
Orange-flower Water.
Lavender Water.
Portugal Water.
Amber Water.
Rose Water.
Hungary Water from Montpelier, &c.

Soaps and Wash-balls.

Amber Washballs.
Bologna Washballs.
Camphir'd Washballs.
Jerusalem Washballs.
Chymical Washballs.
Common Washballs.

Naples Soap.
Jeppa Soap.
Genoa Soap.
Castile or Alicant Soap.
Venice Soap.
Black Soap, &c.

Hair-powders, &c.

Orange-flower Powder.
Amber Perfum'd Powder.
Musk Powder.
Violet Powder.
Rose Powder.
Damask Powder.
Jessamy Powder.
Orrice Powder.
Almond Powder.

Brown and Black Powder.
Fine Plain Powder.
Grounds.
Cypress and Damask Powders, Gross for Sweet Bags,
Linnen, Trunks, &c.

Perfumes, Cosmeticks, Aromaticks, &c.

Ambergrease.
Musk and Civet.
Pulvil.
Balsam Apoplective.
Pearl Powder from India.
Bismuth.
French Red.
Carmine.
A liquid White for the Face.
Spirit of Benjamin.
Portugal Dishes.
Spanish Wool.
All Colours; from China.
Bears Grease.
Almond Paste.
Powder Bags and Boxes.
Powder Puffs of all sorts.
Lip Salve.
Teeth Powder.
Poland Starch.
Common Starch.
Indico and Powder Blues.
Salts for Pocket Bottles.
Sponges.
Perfumes to burn.
Powder Machines.
Boxes for Washballs.
Cases for Oil Bottles, &c.

PLATE 2. Trade card, Charles Lillie, Perfumer at the City of Barcelona, Strand
The British Museum. London

Of the early collectors, Lady Charlotte Schreiber was outstanding. Fortunately she kept a journal, and in this she recorded her finds in the most unexpected places. As early as 1869, at Drey's in Munich, she "made several purchases but not on very advantageous terms — a scent bottle in Venetian glass with flowers £3"; in 1878 in Constantinople she found a Chelsea porcelain bottle, "which the Turk had rased and mounted in silver, leaving it of no value except for the pleasure of buying Chelsea in Constantinople".

Her enthusiasm has been an inspiration to later generations of collectors, who in their turn have encouraged others to share their pleasure in the possession of these delicate objects.

15

PLATE 3. Trade card from Banks Collection
The British Museum, London

The process of making perfume falls roughly into three stages: the selection of raw materials, their preparation and blending, and then the actual making. The raw materials can be divided into two groups, the natural ones and the synthetic. The flowers used for scent are far too numerous for every one to be mentioned, and they come from all over the world — jasmine from Italy, certain roses from Bulgaria, vanilla from Madagascar, and patchouli from India and Singapore. Other flowers used include tuberoses, geranium, lily-of-the-valley, orange flowers, magnolia, oriental flowers, camellia, heliotrope, and gardenia. The main centre for the manufacture of raw materials today is Grasse in Provence, where the selection of

16

these natural products requires great care and knowledge. Flowers, however, are not the only natural ingredients of scent; another important source is to be found in animals, such as the civet cat from Ethiopia and the musk deer from Tibet. Castoreum and ambergris come from the sperm whales. The civet cat must have long been used for this purpose, as can be seen on several eighteenth-century trade cards of perfumers. (Plate 2; other cards are shown on Plates 1, 3.) Synthetic products, developed by chemists, are used by perfumers to complement and extend the use of natural products; thus opening new fields of fragrance.

Once the basic products and ingredients have been selected and properly mixed, they are soaked in alcohol for about six months before being filtered, cooled, and stored until bottled. The high price of perfume today probably arises from the value of the raw materials and the large quantities required to produce quite a small amount of concentrated oils; for instance, to produce one kilogram of concentrated orange, it is necessary to have about 4,500 kilograms of flowers, worth about £2,500. The art of perfume-making undoubtedly lies in the invention of new scents, achieved only rarely, when through experiment and experience a new blend of raw materials is made. "L'eau du Portugal", used by Madame de Pompadour, lasted in popularity for some time, appearing to the public eye as "Tesprit de Portugal distillé", used by Honoré de Balzac.

2 The Beginnings:
Egyptian, Greek & Roman Bottles

THE EGYPTIANS were the first to introduce perfume into civilization, and men and women alike became aware of the pleasure to be found in sweet smells. They used herbs, spices, and scents in their religious lives, and, whether for an everyday occasion or for a more elaborate ceremony, the smell of herbs wafted from the doors of the temples. Incense played a great part in ceremonies of this kind, and flowers and herbs were burned to produce a rich, mellifluous atmosphere. All perfumes at this time were made in the temples, probably by slaves, and were mixed and tested under the supervision of priests; religious processions would wind between temples accompanied by children carrying myrrh, saffron, and incense among other aromatic herbs. Nobles or court favourites who could afford the luxury of a lavish burial were embalmed with cinnamon and myrrh, but this was reserved for the rich alone, as the cost was very high.

The variety of materials used for containers of perfume was perforce rather small. Terracotta and other forms of coarse pottery bottles were quite easy to make, but, because of their small size, great skill and artistry were needed for the intricate detail of their decoration. (Plates 4, 5, 6, 7, 8, 9.) These bottles were mostly of simple form and tended to stimulate precious stones, turquoise and black or pale buff or white ground being the most usual colours. A terracotta bottle in the British Museum is decorated with an invocation to Isis, who travelled the earth searching for fragments of her murdered husband Osiris, and to Amen-Ra, god of the sun, and leading god of the Theban triad: the incised decoration includes a cow in the marshes, symbolic of the goddess Hathor, the goddess

PLATE 4. Terracotta bottle of sphinx form; 6th century B.C. *height 2¼ in. (6.05 cm.)* *The British Museum, London*

PLATE 5. Terracotta scent bottle; 6th century B.C. *height 2¼ in. (6.05 cm.)* *The British Museum, London*

PLATE 6. Terracotta grotesque head bottle; probably Syrian, 6th century B.C. *height 2 in. (5.1 cm.)* *The British Museum, London*

20

PLATE 7. Terracotta warrior's
head scent bottle;
6th century B.C.
height 2 in. (5 1 cm.)
The British Museum, London

PLATE 8. Terracotta unguent pot
of fish form; 6th century B.C
height 2¾ in. (6.05 cm,)
The British Museum London

PLATE 9. Terracotta bottle;
from Camirus in Rhodes,
6th century B.C.
height 2¾ in. (6.65 cm,)
The British Museum, London

PLATE 10. Glass scent bottle;
Egyptian, from Camirus in
Rhodes, 4th-3rd century B.C.
height 3 in (7.65 cm.)
The British Museum, London

of love, who was always depicted with a cow's head. Another bottle, of glazed composition, is inscribed with an invocation to Isis, Amen-Ra, and Ptah (the chief god of Memphis, and the protector of artists and artisans and the inventor· of metal) to grant a happy new year to the owner. Both these vessels were made in the Twenty-sixth Dynasty (*c.* 600 B.C.).

The invention of glass by the Egyptians was a great advance. As early as 4,000 B.C., beads of stone were covered with a form of glaze, which was coloured with a copper compound, thus simulating semi-precious stones; and for a great many years the aim of craftsmen was still to make glass appear like jewels. Glass was first made in the Nile Delta, and Thebes was the chief centre for its production. Alexandria had an active glass trade, and, because the Egyptians were quite rightly proud of their invention, very strict security arrangements surrounded its manufacture to preserve the secret formula; workmen were closely scrutinized both at their work and in their play, a close watch being kept also over the friends with whom they mixed.

Glass was made by the "sand-core" method. (Plates 10, 11.) The opaque glass was heated until it became molten and elastic, and was then wound round a core of sand and clay that had already been

PLATE 11. Sand-core glass
bottle; Egyptian.
2nd-1st century B.C.
height 3 in (7.65 cm.)
The British Museum, London

shaped into the desired form; after that, held with an iron bar, it
was re-heated and tooled, and threads were wound round the bar to
form the neck of the vessel. While still hot, the surface of the bottle
was rolled with brightly-coloured threads, which were then combed
and tooled with metal pins, to produce the desired jewel-like effect.
When the glass had cooled and contracted, and the iron bar had
been removed, the remains of the sand-core were scraped away.
Faults or irregularities were ground down. Handles or feet, which
had been separately modelled, were added, and finally the whole
vessel was heated to fuse the surface and give it a finish. Most of
these vessels were tall and tubular, with short, narrow necks and
bases rather like the end of a test-tube, and they were intended as
containers of unguents, cosmetics, or fragrant oils. From their presence in tombs, it has been widely believed that these bottles were
intended for tears, and, though it is a touching thought that tears
should be preserved with such care, it seems far more probable that
they contained the increasingly popular forms of beauty treatments.

By the fourth century B.C., the nobility had become accustomed
to using perfume daily, and evidence of this can be seen in the
paintings on the walls of tombs. On the wall of the Gardener Tomb
at Thebes, the figures of Sennefera and his wife are seated under the

PLATE 12. Mould-blown glass
bottle; 1st–2nd century A.D.
height 4 in. (10.2 cm.)
The British Museum London

PLATE 13. *(Opposite)*
Mould-blown bottle; Cologne,
2nd–3rd century A.D.
height 6½ in. (16.5 cm.)
The British Museum, London

sacred tree of Amen-Ra, and before them are placed on a table three
jars of perfume. Two of these are conical, with spiral threads; the
third is oviform and has a cylindrical neck.

After the capture of Egypt by the Romans in 27 B.C., Alexandria
still managed to maintain her hold over the glass trade, and
much of the fine glass that was made during the first centuries of
Christianity was manufactured in Egypt; new styles and methods
were developed, but in most aspects of the craft the Roman civilization did no more than follow the ancient Egyptian traditions
of this art.

PLATE 14. *(Opposite)* Attic terracotta scent bottle as bust of Athena; early 4th century B.C *height 7⅞ in. (20 cm.)* *The British Museum, London*

PLATE 15. Helmeted head bottle; Rhodes, 600–540 B.C. *height 2½ in. (6.35 cm.)* *The British Museum London*

PLATE 16. Terracotta crouching monkey; Rhodes, mid 6th century B.C. *height 3¼ in. (7.95 cm.)* *The British Museum, London*

The art of making perfume spread quickly from Egypt to other lands, and Greece became one of the nations most affected by its powers.

Terracotta vessels for perfume appear to have been most popular in Greece. The forms of these bottles reflected aspects of everyday life; some were modelled as women's heads, and were endowed with all the marks of classical beauty. (Plate 14.) Others took the form of a siren, or a soldier's helmeted head, a sandalled foot, or an animal or bird. Many bottles have been found on Rhodes and date from between 600 and 500 B.C. (Plates 15, 16, 17, 18, 19, 20.)

27

PLATE 17. Deer's head bottle; East Greek, perhaps Ionian, second quarter of the 6th century B.C.
height 3⅛ in. (7.95 cm.) The British Museum, London

PLATE 18. Terracotta siren scent bottle; Rhodes, mid 6th century B.C.
height 3⅛ in. (7.95 cm.) The British Museum, London

PLATE I. *(Enlarged)* Mould-blown glass bottle; Roman, Cyprus 1st century A.D.
height 8⅜ in (20.3 cm.) The British Museum, London

PLATE 19. Terracotta sandalled foot; East Greek, second quarter of the 6th
century B.C.
height 3½ in. (8.9 cm.) The British Museum London

PLATE 20. Terracotta bottle as Sphinx; Corinthian, early 6th century B.C.
height 2½ in. (6.35 cm.) The British Museum, London

PLATE II. *(Enlarged)* Opaque-white glass bottle with chinoiserie decoration;
English, 18th century
height 3½ in. (8.9 cm:) Collection Sir Hugh Dawson, London

PLATE 21. Moulded-glass fish bottle; found in France, 1st–2nd century A.D.
length 10 in. (25.4 cm.) The British Museum, London

Glass bottles were also made, largely following the tradition of the Egyptian glass-makers, and small toilet vases made between the sixth and the first century B.C. have been found all over the Mediterranean area (Colour Plate 1, Plates 21, 22), the Nile Delta remaining one of the chief centres, together with the Phoenician coast. Seventh-century glass was of two kinds: transparent glass, which was carved from a solid block of raw glass, and was then shaped and ground; and molten glass, which was taken from a mould and then carved. Some glass was even moulded by the same method as that used for casting bronze. Great progress was made in the design of bottles when it was discovered how to line the mould with sections of thin, multi-coloured glass rods packed side by side, which fused when fired, resulting in the type of glass known today as "millefiori".

The method of moulding glass bottles continued well into the early Roman Imperial period, when society used perfume *ad furorem*. Millefiori and variegated bottles were the most common productions, and these closely resembled certain semi-precious stones; but the moulding process was soon to be eclipsed by the invention of blown glass. Blown glass was invented by the glass-makers of Sidon on the Syrian coast at the end of the first century B.C., and some of the earliest blown-glass vessels bear stamped marks giving the name of the maker and the word "Sidon"; these could have been the experimental productions of a new technique, the makers' names being accompanied by the exhortation: "Buyers, remember!" The method of blowing glass consisted in placing a blob of molten metal on the end of a blow-pipe and inflating it like a balloon. In the early stages, some were blown into moulds as an intermediary process between the easy press-moulding of glass and the more complicated free-blown method.

First-century bottles include a hexagonal example moulded with ewers and vases, a quadrangular bottle with masks, and a faceted bottle; these are similar to others with Medusa masks that have been found with coins of the reign of the Emperor Claudius (A.D. 41-54). They are typical shapes of the period, being often straight-sided and faceted. The glass was mostly coloured — green, blue, or brown; but others were splashed with white spots or feather motifs, again in imitation of the early Egyptian bottles. Many of the glass-blowers deliberately took forms adapted from contemporary pottery (so-called *terra sigillata*); for the classical shapes of Greek pottery long retained their popularity among the Romans.

With the expansion of the Roman Empire under the Emperor Augustus, glass-making spread to Italy and other Mediterranean countries. The River Volturnus appears to have produced a sand as suitable for glass as the River Belus at Sidon had done, and the bottles found at Cumae and Liternum on the Campanian coast of Italy are a good guide. Clearly bottles were highly prized by their owners, and they were evidently objects considered worth stealing; one example made in about 700 B.C. and found at Cumae bears the threat: "I am Tataie's scent bottle — whoever steals me shall go blind".

By the second half of the first century A.D., scent bottles were in

PLATE 22. Blown-glass bottle; Roman Rhineland, 1st–2nd century A.D. *height 5¼ in (13.35 cm.) The British Museum, London*

daily use all over the Roman Empire, and glass factories had sprung up in the western provinces. A particularly successful one was that at Cologne, the richest military city of the north, where the standard of work rivalled the best of the Alexandrians and Syrians. (Plates 12, 13.) The style of glass was somewhat standardized, because craftsmen often came from Egypt or other parts of the Middle East, bringing with them the ancient ideas. Shapes of bottles remained simple, keeping to the classical Greek proportions rather than adopting the elaborate forms of the later Gallic and Syrian types. However, bottles were made also in the form of fruit, including dates or grapes, and others with masks have been found together with coins of the Emperor Constantine and other fourth-century emperors. One type of vessel that has the handles pincered into the form of a dolphin is said to have been suspended from the wrist for use after taking a bath. Similar bottles have been found at Pompeii, but this form, with tooled depressions and pincered ribs, lasted a long time; later examples show cut decoration. Further scent-bottle forms were taken from silver or other metal vessels; colourless glass bottles were made in the Rhineland to simulate the metal ones, the glass being cut with close horizontal grooving. Thick-walled bottles, decorated with circular and oval concavities and circles in counter-sunk relief, are probably of eastern origin, and they anticipate in style the Islamic cut-glass vessels; such examples have been found in Nubia and Fayum on second- and third-century sites, while fourth-century tourist souvenirs have been found at Pozzuoli in Italy.

3 Glass: From the Middle Ages

THE EARLY stages of glass-making having been mastered so successfully by the Egyptians, Greeks, and Romans, it is surprising that,
after the fall of the Roman Empire in the fifth century, glass-
making in Europe should have deteriorated so markedly. During
the seventh and eighth centuries, however, Islamic Egypt revived the
craft: there and in Syria, and throughout the Middle East, vessels
became wild in their proportions as a reaction against the classical
shapes, and even the shapes of scent bottles were modified. While
still molten, they were often decorated with threads of glass, which
became fused together as they were combed upwards spirally, and
so created a barley-sugar effect.

In the ninth century, the Abbasid court moved from Cairo to
Samarra on the River Euphrates. During archaeological excavations
on this site, a variety of objects has been found, including small
scent bottles. Some of these are pear-shaped and of blue or green
glass with thin sides; others have quadrangular bodies, rather heavier
in form, with cut decoration and cylindrical necks. Facet-cutting of
this type has also been found in Old Cairo and elsewhere in Egypt.
Decoration was sometimes engraved, using a technique that was in
practice both by Egyptian and Byzantine craftsmen during the
seventh and eighth centuries. These bottles were widely exported
and have even been found in their original export wrappings.

In the eleventh century, the initiative again passed to Europe,
largely through the trading connections of the Venetians with
Alexandria, where glass had continued to be made since Roman
times. Little is known of the early Venetian experiment, but by the

thirteenth century the island of Murano had become the chief centre of the Venetian glass trade, making coloured beads and vessels. The chronicler Martius da Cavale reports that, on the accession of the Doge Lorenzo Tiepolo in 1268, the Muranese glass-makers carried in procession "rich garlands of beads . . . and decanters and scent bottles and other such glassware". By the end of the century, Venetian glass houses were producing enough to attract foreign buyers and merchants, who came from Germany and other north European countries.

Naturally there were attempts to try to make glass within the city of Venice itself, but the Doge and Senators were afraid that fire might spread from the glass houses into the city. They laid down regulations limiting the size of furnaces, and eventually only small furnaces were permitted. They could not be sited within fifteen yards of any house. This restriction, of course, crippled the trade, and gave a monopoly to the artisans of Murano.

Soon Venetian glass-makers set out from the lagoon and set up glass houses in other north Italian towns — at Bologna, Ferrara, Padua, and Treviso. All these glass houses were restricted by guilds, and the secrets of the craft were carefully guarded.

One of the most successful of these glass houses was that of L'Altare in the marquisate of Montferrat near Genoa, where in the fifteenth century a style called "façon d'Altare" was developed. This closely resembled glass made in Venice. L'Altare was also important because it was not surrounded by the same secrecy; on the contrary, the workers went out from the glass house to spread the knowledge of glass techniques.

The raw material used by the Venetians was made from an ash of plants found on the sea-bed and in the salt marshes, fused with quartz-like pebbles from the Ticino and Po valleys. This produced a very pliable glass, which tended to have a smoky finish. At the same time, before the beginning of the fifteenth century, the Venetians rediscovered the fact that manganese could remove the colour from glass, so they were able to produce a glass bearing a close resemblance to the highly-prized rock crystal. They also continued to make glass in various colours, being — like the Egyptians and Romans — very adept at simulating precious stones. Among the most successfully imitated stones were agate and chalcedony; when aventurine glass was made (simulating a brown sparkling stone), copper particles were mixed in with it to give the glitter of the true stone. Different techniques were also developed for making a millefiori glass.

Few scent bottles can be definitely ascribed to the fifteenth century, but some were copied from pewter or silver shapes with the addition of ribbed trailing in relief, the threads of glass being applied to the bodies and necks while still pliable, then fused and left to cool. In the sixteenth century, shapes were graceful and mostly simple, though at times the clear glass was perfectly trailed with coloured threads, thus finishing the vessel more elaborately. *Latticino* or *lattimo* glass, which could be anything from an opaque creamy-white to a more translucent and delicate glass of watered milky tone, was also used, mixed with clear glass. This style of decoration was especially popular in England and the Netherlands.

Seventeenth-century shapes became much more elaborate. While still pliable, the glass was manipulated and pincered, particularly round the neck, and winged handles were added. The stems of the bottles also took on fanciful shapes.

Through the travels of Venetian glass-makers, their style spread all over Europe. They set up glass houses in the Netherlands and taught the glass-makers of Nuremberg the art of glass-engraving. This was a great speciality of theirs, and one that they had developed themselves. Enamelled glass of Venetian type was made in France and Spain, and this compared quite well with Venetian work. These techniques also spread to Asia, where glass designs combined Venetian with Roman and Islamic influences.

Coloured glass of the seventeenth century was of great elegance, and the same styles continued throughout the following two centuries. The work of the glass-makers in Venice deteriorated to a certain extent during these years, though revivals were attempted. Clever modern reproductions of the early vessels have been produced, and are made in Venice today.

German medieval glass was mostly peasant-made, for domestic use. Much of it came from Bavaria, and flasks and lamps were the most common productions. Most German fifteenth-century shapes were strongly influenced by Venetian glass. Later, in the seventeenth and eighteenth centuries, the use of opaque-white glass — *milchglas,* as it was called — became very well known, and it was frequently decorated with flowers or figure subjects in coloured enamels and gilding; a large number of vessels, including scent bottles, exist of this type. (Plate 23.) Ordinary clear glass bottles were also enamelled, and some of these bear inscriptions. A bottle in the collection of the House of Guerlain bears an inscription and the date 1809. Coloured glass was used in Germany during the sixteenth and seventeenth centuries, but the finest was produced by Johann Kunckel in the last years of the seventeenth century. He was employed by the Great Elector of Saxony, and was hidden away in great secrecy on the Pfauen-Insel near Potsdam, producing his famous ruby glass. A

PLATE 23. Opaque white glass
scent bottle with gilt decoration
and inscription *Il est à vous
SANS Gasconade;* German
height 4¾ in. (12.5 cm.)
*Collection Parfumerie Houbigant,
Paris*

PLATE 24. Louis XIV blue glass
scent bottle, by Bernard Perrot
height 3¾ in. (9.55 cm.)
*Collection Parfumerie Houbigant,
Paris*

certain amount of his glass is mounted in silver, and it is quite likely that there are scent bottles of this kind.

Equally in France, glass-making came under the influence of Italian emigré workers, who formed their own glass houses to gain advantage from the French market. In the sixteenth century Lodovico Gonzaga, who married Henrietta of Cleves and became Duke of Nevers, set up a glass factory at Nevers. This made glass in the Venetian style and was called "Le Petit Murane de Venise" by Thomas Corneille, the younger brother of the dramatist. It produced quantities of small glass figures or "toys". This term, which is frequently found on trade cards, can be defined as small articles such as scent bottles, snuff boxes, étuis, bodkin cases, thimbles and other items to be found on the dressing-table of a lady or a gentleman.

Scent bottles were made in a variety of models, and in the Musée des Arts Decoratifs in Paris are two bottles modelled as boy's heads, one in *verre opaline* of milky tone and the other in black glass.

Colbert, apart from patronizing the Norman glass-makers, supported a certain Bernard Perrot of Orleans, to whom is attributed a group of scent bottles in coloured glass. (Plate 24.) These bottles, generally blue or brown, are moulded in relief with a fleur-de-lis crowned and heart-shaped flowers.

Other Louis XIV scent bottles are made of small coloured *verre eglomisé* beads, and so arranged on a thin glass or ivory ground that they appear at a distance to be in needlework similar to that made at St Cyr in the late sixteenth century. Several of remarkable quality are in the Musée des Arts Decoratifs in Paris, decorated with such motifs as a coat of arms, Venus drawn in a chariot, and exotic birds. They have most attractive colours and, like the bottle illustrated, a flattened form. (Plate 25.) The use of this form was continued in the reign of Louis XV. (Plate 26.)

Glass was also made in Normandy, Lorraine, Picardy, Lyons, and Provence; here there was a progressive attitude to the development of new techniques, while the traditional *verre de fougère* or peasant-made green soda-glass continued to be made. During Colbert's ministry, in the early days of Louis XIV, the art of making plate glass for mirrors was discovered in Normandy; this was of particular importance because previously it had been made only in Venice and Nuremberg. Colbert brought the Norman craftsmen to Paris and set up a royal glass house in 1675, producing sheets of glass of unprecedented size and quality.

The Egyptians, and indeed many of their followers, had decorated glass by splashing it with various colours; the Venetians had also

PLATE 25. *(Opposite) "Verre eglomise"* bottle simulating needlework, inscribed *Il Plait à l'Oeil et Flatte l'Odorat;* French, 17th century *height 6 in (15.25 cm.)* *Collection Parfumerie Houbigant, Paris*

PLATE 26. A Louis XV gold-mounted glass bottle bearing marks of Jacques Meyboon and the Paris discharge mark for 1732–38 *height 4⅛ in. (10.45 cm.)* *Collection Claude Leigh, London*

used this technique, and under their influence the French glass-makers decorated some of their scent bottles in this way, the glass being splashed with brilliant tones of red, yellow, blue, and white. Some seventeenth-century bottles that are shaped as *tonnelets*, or barrels, have this kind of decoration. The technique continued throughout the eighteenth and nineteenth centuries, and was pro-duced in a different form by the glass houses at Baccarat, Clichy, and St Louis. The factory at Baccarat, near Lunéville in north-eastern France, was founded in 1765, and, though conventional glass was produced here, the factory is probably now best known for its production of paper-weights, which began about 1845. Here the millefiori technique was a speciality, and scent bottles and flasks with a heavy base of this type are well known.

Little, however, is known about the early glass-makers in England. Norman artisans set up glass houses in the Weald, and made the same kind of peasant soda-glass as was made in Germany and France.

39

Towards the end of the sixteenth century, Protestants from Lorraine arrived in England, and they brought with them a knowledge of glass that ensured a great technical improvement among the English makers. One of these Lorrainers, Carré, set himself up at Crutched Friars, London, in 1567, and can justifiably claim the honour of having established glass-making of a high quality in England. As a result of protests from the Wealden glass-makers, Carré's workmen dispersed; eventually they established the glass houses of Stourbridge and Newcastle-upon-Tyne. Carré died in 1572. Jacopo Verzellini, a Venetian who had come to London from Antwerp in 1575, was able to benefit from the valuable work done by Carré and to continue what Carré had begun but had been unable to carry through. Verzellini obtained permission from Queen Elizabeth to set up a workshop for making Venetian glasses; moreover, he secured a royal licence prohibiting the import of any foreign glasses. This gave a chance for the native trade to develop. Fewer than ten drinking glasses or bowls definitely attributable to Verzellini have survived, but those that have can be identified by their diamond-point engraving ascribed to a Frenchman, Anthony de Lysle.

A century later, in 1675, the Glass Sellers Company, which was attached to a city guild, employed George Ravenscroft as chief glass-maker and researcher to provide a substitute for the Venetian glass. The English trade in glass had been hampered because much of it, when exported, arrived damaged; what was required was a metal glass that would combine strength with clarity. Another difficulty in making glass was the "crizzling" or decomposition of the glass, a disease that gave rise to the term "sick" glass. It appeared that the introduction of lead into the molten body considerably lessened this crizzling. Ravenscroft gradually perfected this mixture, so that by 1682, when Hawley Bishopp officially took over Ravenscroft's Savoy glass house, the new "flint" glasses, as these lead glasses were called, had reached full production.

From then on large quantities of excellent drinking glasses were made, and in the late seventeenth century and throughout the eighteenth century the English glass-makers concentrated on drinking glasses, decanters, and other glass vessels for domestic use.

Perhaps the mid-eighteenth-century glass best known by name is the one called after Bristol, where its manufacture was closely related to experiments in porcelain-making. In 1750 a factory making porcelain from soapstone was established in Bristol at a glass house owned by a William Lowdin and situated at Redcliffe Backs. At about the same time opaque-white glass vessels, including.

PLATE 27. Blue glass bottle with
gold mount Bristol, circa 1760
height 3¼ in. (8.25 cm.)
Collection Claude Leigh, London

PLATE 28. Amethyst glass bottle;
Bristol, circa 1760
height 3 in. (7.65 cm.)
Collection Claude Leigh, London

enamelled scent bottles, were produced in Bristol, and they continued to be made until the end of the eighteenth century. There
are also facet-cut bottles of the same type, but made in clear glass,
in translucent blue glass (which is normally thought of as "Bristol"
glass), in an emerald green glass, and in an unusual translucent
violet or amethyst glass. (Plates 27, 28.) At the sale of the William
Edkins Collection of porcelain and glass in 1874, Lot 126 is described
as "Another pair [of bottles] in white enamel, £1 10s.", the glass
being made by Little & Longman & Successors on Redcliffe Backs
Bristol between 1750 and 1770.

Scent bottles of this type are sometimes entirely plain, but various
forms of decoration appear on others. Usually the ornament is in the
form of delicately gilded floral sprays or birds, or rococo scrolls
enclosing figures of Chinamen or animals. Others are decorated with
delicate, coloured enamels, the designs being often repeated.
The most characteristic scenes are all painted by the same hand —
for example, a church in the foreground with swimming and
swooping ducks on the reverse. It is usual to find a bouquet of

41

PLATE 29. Opaque-white glass
bottle with coloured flowers:
south Staffordshire, perhaps
Birmingham
height 3 in. (7.65 cm.)
Courtesy Sotheby & Co., London

flowers; often this centres round the particular detail of a rose.
Billing doves are also shown, and so are figures of gallants and
ladies, lovers and small Chinamen. The finest are the opaque-white
bottles with brilliant enamel painting, possibly by the enigmatic
Michael Edkins, or by some other independent enameller, such as
James Giles of Kentish Town, who was recognized for his decoration

PLATE 30. Two blue glass bottles
with gilt chinoiseries in
original shagreen case
height 2 in. (5.1 cm.)
Tilley and Co., London

PLATE 31. Cut glass commemor-
ative bottle; Bristol
height 3 ⅞ in. (9.85 cm.)
Collection Richard Dennis

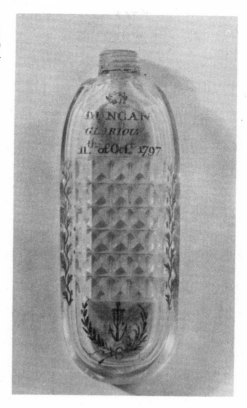

on Bow, Chelsea, and Worcester porcelain. It is likely that Edkins,
who is known to have been an enameller on glass at Bristol, painted
the decoration of birds and tightly-arranged bouquets of flowers,
while the chinoiserie designs (Colour Plate II) were carried out by
independent enamellers and painters more often employed in decorating salt-glazed pottery made as far away as Fenton Low, Tunstall,
and Shelton in Staffordshire, and even at Leeds and Liverpool.

The coloured glass, particularly the blue, so often attributed to
Bristol may well have been made in the Birmingham and South
Staffordshire areas. (Plates 29, 30.) It is conceivable that it was
brought to London, to be painted, enamelled, and mounted by
jewellers and goldsmiths; a close proximity is evident between the
painting on certain scent bottles of this kind and on some watch
cases decorated and mounted in London.

Articles for the everyday use of ladies were advertised and sold
throughout the country. In 1766 "Ladies' Dressing-Boxes and Sweet

Water Bottles for the Ladies' Toilets" were advertised "from the stock-in-trade of a German who was the first that brought the Art of Cutting and Engraving of Glass from Germany"! This German is said to have been a certain Haedy, a Bohemian cutter who worked in London during the last quarter of the eighteenth century.

Dated glass scent bottles are rather rare, though an opaque-white facet-cut bottle in the Dawson collection is inscribed with the name and date "William Coventry 1777", and two other bottles in the same collection are inscribed respectively "JL 1785" and "TN 1785". When the Trapnell collection was sold in 1912, one item was listed as a "Scent Bottle, deep blue borders, painted with a bunch of forget-me-nots on one side, on the other with initials and date S.B. 1799 surrounded with green and blue ornament, 2½ in." Another facet-cut glass scent bottle commemorates the victory of the English fleet, commanded by Admiral Duncan, over the Dutch, and bears an anchor surrounded by a laurel wreath, below a laurel crown and the inscription "DUNCAN GLORIOUS 11th of Octr, 1797". (Plate 31.)

Excise duties limited the production of glass in England during the late eighteenth century, and this coincided with the grant to Ireland of free trade. The production of Irish glass was thus encouraged, and it was exported not only to America but also to England. During this period much cut glass was produced in Dublin, Waterford, Cork, and Belfast; but it is difficult to assign pieces of glass to definite Irish glass houses. Few scent bottles can be identified as Irish.

Scent bottles were also produced at Nailsea, near Bristol, during the nineteenth century, and at Stourbridge. The latter productions were very similar to those made at the French factories of Baccarat and St Louis. Massive scent bottles were made with millefiori canes forming the base, while others were striped in brilliant colours.

As might be expected, Lady Charlotte Schreiber also collected glass scent bottles. On the 3rd of October 1882, at Haarlem in Holland, she records the following find: "4 hours. were regretting our loss of time and trouble, when, as a sort of forlorn hope, we looked into Leeuw's where we never yet found anything to buy, and our eyes were greeted with the sight of the loveliest of smelling bottles of fine Bristol glass! I need not say that I carried it off in triumph to add to the three other little darlings that I have at home"

PLATE III. Enamel bottle with gold mounts; German, Fromery workshop
(Enlarged)   height 3¼ in. (8.25 cm.) Collection Parfumerie Houbigant, Paris

4 Enamel Bottles

THE EARLIEST mention of *champlevé* enamelling appears about A.D. 240 in the works of the sophist Philostratus, who wrote (*Eikones* I, 28): "It is said that the barbarians in the ocean pour these colours into bronze moulds, that the colours become as hard as stone, preserving the designs". Enamel is made from a vitreous substance, but the description of the technique is not altogether correct; *champlevé* enamelling is done by scooping out troughs or holes in the metal, leaving tiny walls between the hollows, which when filled with liquid enamel is then fused. Afterwards the whole surface is filed and smoothed with a pumice stone, and polished with crocus-powder and rouge.

At the beginning of the fourteenth century the *baisse-taille* technique was developed. This required a high standard of crafts-manship both in the handling of the enamel and in the preparation of the metal. The gold or silver ground was engraved with the intended design, which was then chiselled out in the manner of a seal. The enamel was poured into the cavities, filling them so that the decoration was level with the metal outlines, the engraved design showing through the translucent enamel.

This technique was used to decorate ecclesiastical vessels, including candlesticks, crosses, book covers, and plate, and was particularly favoured by the French goldsmiths.

PLATE IV. *(Enlarged)* Enamel double-gourd bottle; German, mid 17th century *height 2 in. (5.1 cm.) Collection Claude Leigh, London*

PLATE 32 Enamel fish scent bottle; Italian, 17th century
Kunsthistorisches Museum. Vienna

The *cloisonné* technique was invented at about the same time, but it was mainly used in China and Japan. Cells for the enamel were built up by placing thin strips of metal in the shape of the design on a metal plate. The strips were fixed by the enamel itself or by silver solder, and the enamel was then fused, the finishing process being the same as that used in the *champlevé* enamel technique. In China, the best work in *cloisonné* enamel was made during the Ming Dynasty (1342-1643) and the Ch'ing Dynasty (1644-1912); later it became much debased.

The fourth and final method of enamelling, which for the scent bottle is the most important, is that of painted enamelling. Among the problems of producing enamel, one of the most difficult was to make it adhere to a thin plate. The solution was discovered in the early sixteenth century, probably by the Venetians, and consisted in covering both sides of the metal plate with a coat of the same enamel, so that, when fired, the two coats would shrink together, holding the metal between them. This coating formed the ground on which any subsequent decoration was carried out. The metal used for this process was generally copper, gold, or silver. The completed article was finished with a mount in the same material.

By the seventeenth century, enamelling was done all over Europe, and among the objects decorated with it was the scent bottle. In Italy goldsmiths flourished, and a variety of objects were made demonstrating the scope of the enameller's art. In the Kunsthistorisches Museum in Vienna there is an enamelled scent bottle in the form of a reticulated fish (Plate 32) this was probably made in Italy during the seventeenth century. The shape was also popular for other things, a sale catalogue at Christie's mentions a "silver jointed fish étui" from the "Stock in Trade of Mr. James Cox, of Shoe-Lane, Jeweller" for the 16th and 17th of December 1772, as part of a lot entitled "Various articles for a ladies toilet".

A bottle was purchased by Lady Charlotte Schreiber in Breslau on the 25th of July 1876. She notes in her journal: "Before leaving Breslau to-day, we walked back to Altmann's to get a little Cinque-cento enamelled flacon I had seen there and coveted. I fancy it is one of those with a double side, which was in those days used for poisonous scents".

Berlin was one of the main centres of the enamelling craft during the early part of the eighteenth century, and among the decorators

PLATE 33. Enamel bottle with chinoiseries; Berlin, 18th century
height 2⅝ in. (6.65 cm.)
Collection Parfumerie Houbigant, Paris

PLATE 34. Enamel combined scent bottle and watch case; French, 17th century
height 2¼ in. (5.7 cm.)
Collection Claude Leigh, London

were Christoph Conrad Hunger and Alexander Fromery, who both produced work of a rare quality and of excellent design. They must have worked in close co-operation with the gold and silversmiths of the day, as can be seen by the high quality of the gold mounts to the Berlin bottle decorated with landscapes. (Colour Plate III, Plate 33.) Other work of this kind was done at Augsburg, another centre of workers in gold and silver.

French craftsmen used enamelling to decorate such multi-purpose objects as a scent bottle fitted to enclose a watch, despite the dangers involved to the movement. (Plate 34.) This bottle has been painted on the lid, in the manner of the Huault brothers, with figures surmounted by a border painted with flowers. Copied after engravings by David Teniers the younger, it dates from the late seventeenth century; so does the double-gourd bottle painted with a *mille-fleurs* design, conceivably the work of a German or Dutch craftsman. (Colour Plate IV, Plate 35.) Some of the northern European enamel work is reminiscent of English enamels made in Staffordshire in the eighteenth century. Lazare Duvaux, the notable "marchand bijoutier", notes in his journal for the 2nd of January 1753: "Received from Mme. the Marquise de Pompadour, in payment by the hands of Monsieur de Montmartel, the sum of 14,116L plus a two-piece *étui* and an enamel flacon taken back that I had sold, one at 146L, the other at 180L, total 336L".

There is a general misapprehension that all English enamels were made at Battersea. But, the Battersea enamel factory, which was founded in 1753 by Sir Stephen Theodore Janssen, survived only for three years, when it was closed on account of Janssen's bankruptcy. During this short period, it is probable that only a few of the best-quality enamels were produced. Among these are some fine transfer-printed enamels by Robert Hancock, Simon-François Ravenet, and Jean Pillement, but there is no mention in the contemporary records of any scent bottles having been made at Battersea. It is possible that some independent porcelain decorators at work in London may have done some enamel work as a sideline, and scent bottles may well have formed part of their stock. (Plate 36.) Trade cards specifically mention the presence of "enamelled toys", and men at work in London in the 1750s under the title of "enamblers" included Daniel Campbell of St Sepulchre, Middlesex; Joseph Briddle of St Giles, Whitechapel; Samuel Smith of St Bride's; and Joseph Pope of High Holborn.

The largest centre of the enamelling trade was in and around Bilston in Staffordshire. It was within easy reach of Birmingham,

PLATE 35. Silver-mounted enamel
bottle; German
height 3 in. (7.65 cm.)
Collection Parfumerie Houbigant,
Paris

PLATE 36. A London-decorated
enamel scent bottle
height 1⅜ in. (4.1 cm.)
Winifred Williams Antiques
Eastbourne

49

PLATE 37. Enamel Squirrel scent bottle; Staffordshire *height 2⅞ in. (7.3 cm.)* *Collection the late the Hon. Mrs Nellie Ionides*

where there were manufacturers of metal mounts, among them the celebrated firm of Boulton and Fothergill. One of the best Birmingham enamellers was undoubtedly John Taylor, a pioneer in cheap enamel bibelots with copper-gilt mounts. He was also a partner in a flint-glass house at Stourbridge, and probably produced the same kind of objects in glass. Apart from decorating his enamel bibelots with painted scenes, it is probable that Taylor employed Robert Hancock, the well-known transfer-printer who worked at the Battersea enamel factory and for several of the porcelain factories, more especially Bow and Worcester. In 1759 Taylor remarked: "There are two or three drawing schools established in Birmingham for the Instruction of youth in the Arts of Drawing and Designing, and thirty or forty Frenchmen are constantly employed in drawing and designing". Numbers of French craftsmen, who are known to have worked in London on porcelain modelling and decoration, travelled north and were largely responsible for the attempts of the midland artisans to start producing enamels locally. It appears that Taylor was not a particularly generous or keen employer, for in 1775 James Watt wrote to Matthew Boulton, of the Birmingham metal works, that "John Taylor died the other day worth £200,000 without ever doing one generous action". Similar enamels were made at Wednesbury near Birmingham, sharing the benefits of the metal trade. Here Margaret and William Bielby, the glass-enamellers, were apprenticed, before they went to Newcastle-upon-Tyne.

Of the Bilston enamellers, one of the best known was Dovey Hawksford, who died in 1749. He evidently pursued several professions in the course of his life, but he must have begun acquiring his knowledge of the enamel trade in the early years of the eighteenth century. It is known that a William Homer of Walsall was apprenticed to him as early as 1722, and the Homer brothers are known to have been painters on enamel in the Bilston area. Hawksford, however, was described in 1741 as a chapman or itinerant vendor, but presumably his wares were in fact his own enamels. Another person mentioned in connection with the manufacture of enamel is Benjamin

PLATE 38. Enamel combined scent bottle and bonbonnière; Staffordshire, printed and painted design adapted from Robert Hancock, blue ground height 3½ in. (8.9 cm.) Collection Lord Ilford, London

PLATE 39. Enamel bottle of
Rococo form; Staffordshire
height 3¾ in. (9.85 cm.)
Collection the late the Hon.
Mrs Nellie Ionides

PLATE 40. Combined scent bottle
and bonbonnière; Staffordshire
height 3 in. (7 65 cm.)
Collection the late the Hon.
Mrs Nellie Ionides

Bickley, a "toy"-maker who in 1741 was accepted as an apprentice by Joshua S. Devey. The Devey family were toy-makers in Wolverhampton as early as 1729.

The decoration on English enamels made in the Bilston and Birmingham areas does not vary considerably. (Plates 37, 38, 39, 40.) The same scenes and subjects crop up on scent bottles, étuis, bodkin cases, or snuff boxes. At times porcelain models were copied, as for instance in a bottle that has the form of billing doves. Pastoral scenes with lovers were embodied, in a style reminiscent of Watteau. Landscapes and flowers are seen; these last may well have been taken from books of designs such as the *Ladies Amusement* by Robert Sayer. Another method of decoration was to paint a scent bottle with a portrait after an engraving. One instance of this is the portrait

PLATE 41. Three enamel scent bottles; Staffordshire, 18th century
height 3 in. — 4¼ in. (7.65 cm. — 10.45 cm.) Collection Claude Leigh, London

of Miss Anne (Nancy) Day, afterwards Lady Fenhoulet, from an engraving possibly by Purcell after the portrait by Sir Joshua Reynolds. This portrait also appears on an étui in the Schreiber Collection at the Victoria and Albert Museum, though it is possible that the engraving is carried out by James McArdell, Reynolds's more usual engraver. Most of these different types of decoration were made on a coloured ground with gilt scroll borders to the rococo panels, and often with white enamel diaper or florettes on the ground. (Plate 41.) To produce the right texture of gilding, the crushed gold leaf had to be mixed with honey — a fact that must have encouraged the bee-keepers of the district.

Many of these enamel bottles and other small necessities for a lady's dressing-table were exported and became popular all over Europe. In Amsterdam in 1874, Lady Charlotte Schreiber in her indefatigable way managed to find what she wanted: "At Sonjet's we bought a pretty Battersea smelling bottle, of two doves — very much à la Chelsea".

There are still many French forgeries in circulation. These were made mainly by the fastidious M. Emile Samson, who was working in Paris at the end of the last century. However, it requires only a modicum of knowledge to distinguish these from genuine ones, the chief clues being that his enamelling and gilding are rather coarse.

5 Chelsea & 'Girl in a Swing' Bottles

IT IS EVIDENT from the large numbers of Chelsea "toys" known today that they must have been very popular in the eighteenth century. However, to attribute all this success to the Chelsea porcelain factory is misleading, for the toys, and particularly the scent bottles, were clearly not all made by the same hand.

The first mention in print of a porcelain factory in England was made in a petition from the Vincennes porcelain factory to Louis XV in 1745, where it is mentioned that "a new establishment which has just been formed in England, of a factory making porcelain which appears to be more beautiful than that made at Meissen". This was high praise indeed from one of Europe's foremost centres of porcelain-production, and the establishment referred to in such a complementary manner can only be assumed to be that at Chelsea.

Apparently it was founded in 1745 by Charles Gouyn, a French jeweller and porcelain-dealer, in partnership with Nicholas Sprimont, a Flemish silversmith. Their first productions were based on Sprimont's silver shapes, and the material used was very experimental. In 1749 Gouyn and Sprimont split up. Sprimont obtained new financial support from Sir Everard Falkner, secretary to the Duke of Cumberland, and continued to run the Chelsea factory until, through ill health, he was forced to sell it to William Duesbury of Derby. All that was lacking in the early days of the factory was royal patronage, which had been the key to the success of most continental porcelain factories. Instead of continuing to model porcelain after his own silver designs, Sprimont was now persuaded to branch out and follow more closely what was going on in foreign porcelain factories. Here Falkner was useful, for he was a friend of the Ambassador to the Saxon Court at Dresden, Sir Charles Hanbury Williams, who lent him his collection of Meissen figures that was stored at Holland House, Kensington, so that Sprimont could study their modelling and make copies of them. However, few direct copies were made during the early Chelsea periods, and inspiration tended to come from other sources, such as contemporary sculpture and Chinese "blanc-de-Chine" figures. Among these the best-known subjects are Kuan Yin (the goddess of mercy) and Pu Tai (the corpulent monk seated with his bag of wind).

The presence in England in the 1750s of celebrated sculptors, including François Roubiliac, Peter Scheemakers, and Michael Rysbrack, encouraged porcelain factories to produce figures with a topical attraction. Much of the freshness in the modelling of these portrait busts and full-length figures is due to Huguenot workmen, some of whom had worked in factories in their own country. The most important of these was undoubtedly Joseph Willems, a fellow-countryman of Sprimont, and a modeller of figures who went to Chelsea about 1749 and was the first to give its products a distinct style. His work branched away from the somewhat stylized modelling of both the Meissen-type figures and of Sprimont's other early attempts, and took on a more rustic and homely appearance that was more suitable to the medium in which he was working.

Meanwhile Gouyn, though he had left the Chelsea porcelain factory, continued to be actively interested in porcelain-making. It has been suggested that he may have backed a group of Staffordshire potters. According to a story by Simeon Shaw, published in his *History of the Staffordshire Potteries* (1829), they had gone to work at the Chelsea China Manufactory in 1747, and soon finding themselves responsible for all the good work produced there, determined to set up in business on their own somewhere in Chelsea. They had a fair success, and for this they would have needed financial support. As there is no evidence of where they acquired it, perhaps Gouyn was the source. Moreover, the proprietor of the Chelsea China Warehouse, a certain S. Stables, claimed that he had goods made by Gouyn.

The first mention of a public sale of Chelsea porcelain appears in the *Public Advertiser* from the 29th of March to the 26th April 1754. Unfortunately no catalogue of this sale has yet been discovered, and in the announcement of the sale no mention is made of the inclusion of any porcelain "toys". However, from the 23rd of November to the 21st of December 1754, the *Public Advertiser* announced a five day sale in the following terms:

By Order of the Proprietors of the Chelsea Porcelain
Manufactory

To be Sold by Auction
by MR. FORD
At his great Room in St. James' Haymarket on Monday the
16th December and the following days

All the entire Stock of PORCELAIN TOYS, brought from

their Warehouse in Pall Mall;

consisting of Snuff boxes, Smelling Bottles, Etwees and

(mounted in gold, and unmounted) in various beautiful

Shapes, of an elegant

Design, and curiously painted in Enamel.

The said Stock may be view'd, and Catalogue had, at
Mr. Ford's on Wednesday the 11th of December, and the
following Days, Sunday excepted till the Time of Sale, which
will begin each Day at half an Hour after Eleven o'clock.

Nothing of the above kind was in their former Sale, nor
will any Thing of the same Sort as in this be sold from the
Manufactory till after next year.

The advertisement further points out that "Most of the above
things are in lots suitable for Jewellers, Goldsmiths, Toy-shops,
China-shops, Cutlers, and Workmen in these Branches of Business".

As Mr Robert Charleston and the late Mr Arthur Lane pointed
out in their paper to the English Ceramic Circle in 1960, nowhere
does the advertisement mention that the "toys" were made by the
"Chelsea Porcelain Manufactory", but only that they were "brought
from their Warehouse in Pall-Mall". Mr J. E. Nightingale published
a signed announcement by Nicholas Sprimont; it appeared in the
Daily Advertiser of the 15th of May 1750, and declared that the
warehouse at the factory would be open for viewing the new productions. It added the following statement: "Note, The Quality and
Gentry may be assured, that I am not concern'd in any Shape whatsoever with the goods exposed to Sale in St. James's Street, called
the Chelsea-China Warehouse".

In reply to this surprising statement, there exists the following
announcement in the *General Advertiser* of the 17th of January 1750:

57

PLATE 42. "Girl in a Swing"
hawk scent bottle
height 2¾ in. (7 cm.)
Collection of Mrs Meyer Sassoon

PLATE 43. "Girl in a Swing"
scent bottle as a cat with a
mouse
height 3 in. (7.65 cm.)
Collection of Mrs Meyer Sassoon

PLATE 44. "Girl in a Swing"
Cochin-china cock and a rooster
height 2¾ in. (7 cm.)
Collection of Mrs Meyer Sassoon

PLATE 45. "Girl in a Swing" boy
with a bird and a dalmatian scent
bottle
height 2⅝ in. (6.65 cm.)
Collection of Mrs Meyer Sassoon

Chelsea China Warehouse

SEEING it frequently advertised, that the Proprietor of Chelsea Porcelaine is not concerned in any shape whatsoever in the Goods exposed to Sale in St. James's Street, called the Chelsea China Warehouse, in common Justice to N. Sprimont, (who signed the Advertisement) as well as myself, I think it incumbent, publickly to declare to the Nobility, Gentry &c that my China Warehouse is not supply'd by any other person than Mr. Charles Gouyn, late Proprietor and Chief Manager of the Chelsea-House, who continues to supply me with the most curious Goods of that Manufacture, as well useful as ornamental, and which I dispose of at very reasonable Rates.

. S. Stables

Chelsea China Warehouse,
St. James's Street, Jan
17th, 1750

All these public statements and refutations lead one to suppose that Gouyn and his Staffordshire potters succeeded in establishing a reasonably successful porcelain factory somewhere in Chelsea, and that they were responsible for the so-called "girl in a swing".

The name was derived from a figure depicting a girl swinging on a seat hung between two branches, and though the identity of the unmistakable modeller of the scent bottles and other toys made at

PLATE 46. "Girl in a Swing" scent bottle; Gouyn factory, Rococo shape
height 1½ in. (3.8 cm.)
Winifred Williams Antiques, Eastbourne

the factory has yet to be discovered, they evidently spring from the same source. (Plates 42, 43, 44, 45.) There are various other related figures and groups, but so far the nearest approach to a "ware" that can be attributed to the factory is the miniature chest containing glass scent bottles. (Colour Plate V.) All these have characteristic enamel decoration.

The scent bottles associated with these Chelsea factories are of five types.

The first group, which appears to be the smallest in number, consists of bottles of exceptionally fine quality. (Plate 46.) The models, which measure not more.than four inches, include a tall Chinaman (Plate 47) and a similar figure of a Chinese lady, another of a lady holding a basket in front of her; a girl with a hurdy-gurdy (Plate 48); a dancing girl, with a sleeping girl watched over by a woebegone mastiff; billing doves; Harlequin, a swan; a rooster; a parrot with a Cochin-china cock; a pug; and a cat.

PLATE 48. "Girl in a Swing"
lady with a hurdy-gurdy;
Gouyn factory
height 3½ in. (8.9 cm.)
Courtesy Sotheby & Co., London

PLATE 49. Scent bottle in the
form of a frightened Harlequin
height 2¾ in. (7 cm.)
Collection Mrs Meyer Sassoon

PLATE 50. "Girl in a Swing" type
Harlequin and Rose scent bottle
height 3½ in. (8.9 cm.)
Collection Parfumerie Houbigant,
Paris

All these bear the same characteristics: a greyish paste; sharply modelled features; grey hair; clothes decorated with sprays of mixed garden flowers; a bunch of cherries; leaves of yellow-green with brown tinges; brown tree-trunks; and a spray of mixed garden flowers on the underside. They are finished with good gold mounts worthy of a jeweller. It is this group that can definitely be assigned to Gouyn and the girl-in-a-swing factory.

The next group, which consists of a greater number of models, has certain distinct characteristics. The figures have chocolate-brown hair depicted in carefully drawn brush-strokes; their eyes are outlined in the same colour; the clothes and bases are decorated with a somewhat mean-looking single pink rose, which is repeated on the underside of the base; the supports have green and turquoise-green leaves and no trunk; often the figures are seated on green marble plinths; and the bases are inscribed with mottoes (a feature that does not appear on the bottles in the first group). The colouring of different examples of the same model is often identical, and includes a particularly brilliant turquoise, which does not appear on bottles in other groups;

63

PLATE 51. "Girl in a Swing"
type soldier scent bottle
height 2½ in. (6.35 cm.)
Collection Parfumerie Houbigant,
Paris

PLATE 52. "Girl in a Swing"
type gallant scent bottle
height 3¼ in. (8.25 cm.)
Collection Parfumerie Houbigant,
Paris

often the underside of the base is decorated with a border of alternating green and turquoise-green leaves. The paste used is glassy and brittle, and the gold mounts are of indifferent quality. The most usual models found are a seated girl picking grapes into a basket; a man with his arms around a girl standing against a rose tree; the sleeping girl with a mastiff (distinctly smaller in size than that in the previous group); Venus and Cupid with a clock; a girl standing with a dove in her hands and a spotted dog at her side; Harlequin offering Columbine a slice of melon; Cupid at a furnace; Cupid with a bow and arrows; Cupid at a fountain; a Chinese family; a billing-doves bottle (also smaller than that in the previous group); and a pug dog. An outstandingly good bottle is that of a hussar. (Colour Plate VI.) It is more than curious that the distinguishing features of

65

PLATE 54. A pineapple bottle;
Chelsea, red anchor period
height 2⅞ in. (7.3 cm.)
Collection Mrs Meyer Sassoon

PLATE 55. A peacock bottle;
Chelsea red anchor period
height 3½ in. (8.9 cm.)
Collection Mrs Meyer Sassoon

this group should be so strong, and, though any concrete evidence has yet to be discovered, I would suggest that perhaps these bottles were not made either at the girl-in-a-swing factory or at Sprimont's Chelsea factory, but at some allied concern. (Plates 50, 51, 52.)

The third group consists of those bottles that are undoubtedly of Sprimont's Chelsea "red-anchor" period and probably date from about 1755. (Plates 53, 54, 55, 56.) A large number of these are animal and bird subjects, and they may well have been taken from engravings by Pillement and other masters printed for Robert Sayer in the *Ladies Amusement*, London, 1762. (Plates 57, 58, 59, 60, 61.) They include a hen and her chickens; a squirrel and her young; entwined dolphins; fish in a net; a duck and her ducklings; a pug; various vases of flowers and bouquets; tulip blooms; a few clusters of plums, cherries, and other fruit; a series of monks and nuns, and the amusing "Provender for a Monastery"; and a few bottles depicting scenes from the illustrations to Barlow's fables. (Plates 62, 65.) All these have typical red-anchor painting, and have gilt dentil rims to the bases, with characteristic large sprays of flowers on the underside.

PLATE 56. A cat scent bottle;
Chelsea, red anchor period
height 3 in. (7.65 cm.)
Collection Mrs Meyer Sassoon

PLATE 57. A monkey bottle;
Chelsea, red anchor period
height 2½ in. (6.35 cm.)
Collection Parfumerie Houbigant,
Paris

PLATE 58. A fish bottle;
Chelsea, red anchor period
height 3¾ in. (9.55 cm.)
Collection Parfumerie Houbigant,
Paris

PLATE 59. A swan; Chelsea, red
anchor period
height 2¼ in. (5.7 cm.)
Collection Parfumerie Houbigant,
Paris

PLATE 60. A monk bottle; Chelsea,
red anchor period
height 3½ in. (8.9 cm.)
Collection Parfumerie Houbigant,
Paris

PLATE 61. A bottle with two
stoppers, depicting Portia;
Chelsea, red anchor period
height 3½ in. (8.9 cm.)
Courtesy Sotheby & Co., London

PLATE 62. A fable bottle, "The
Fox and the Raven"; Chelsea,
red anchor period
height 3⅛ in. (7.95 cm.)
Collection Parfumerie Houbigant,
Paris

70

PLATE 63. A Janus head bottle;
Chelsea, gold anchor period
height 3¾ in. (9.55 cm.)
Collection Mrs Meyer Sassoon

PLATE 64. A bottle depicting
Cupid as a sculptor; Chelsea,
gold anchor period
height 3¼ in. (8.25 cm.)
Collection Mrs Meyer Sassoon

PLATE 65. A fable bottle,"The Fox and the Stork"; Chelsea, gold anchor period
height 4 in. (10.15 cm.)
Collection Mrs Meyer Sassoon

There is another group of bottles, which, though small in number, is of curious interest. These bottles have usually been attributed to Sprimont's Chelsea factory, but there has always been a certain doubt about them. I suggest that they have nothing to do with Chelsea but derive from Meissen figures. (Plate 49.) Their subjects are usually taken from the Commedia dell'Arte, depicting Harlequin with a rooster, and a monkey on the other side of the tree; Harlequin singing; or Harlequin with sprawling limbs and wide-open mouth, together with a squirrel and a rooster. All are unmarked, except one in the Untermeyer Collection that bears a gold-anchor mark. They are of soft-paste porcelain, but rather larger than the Chelsea bottles, and are very light in weight. They have little resemblance in subject-matter and composition to the usual bottles of the gold-anchor period to which they are supposed to correspond in date, and I am inclined to

PLATE 66. A bottle depicting
Orpheus and lute; Chelsea,
gold anchor period
height 4 in. (10.15 cm.)
Collection Parfumerie Houbigant,
Paris

think that they are by a highly imaginative copyist, possibly at work in the eighteenth century, or the first half of the nineteenth.

The "gold-anchor" Chelsea scent bottles form the fifth group. (Plates 63, 64.) They have figures very similar to those of other bottles made in the same period (1758–63). The figures are in fact often taken from the models that were used for the earlier bottles, but the later decoration is distinctive. Models include a seated spinning maiden; a young boy offering a bouquet to a girl; Cupid with a lion; Cupid with an ass; a series of Aesop's fables; shepherds with sheep; and many with very childish boys at various pursuits. The bases are sometimes washed with green and have a large gilt spray on the underside. They are all more richly adorned than their predecessors and are particularly different from them in that they bear the addition of much gilding. (Plate 66.)

PLATE 67. A heart-shaped crimson
ground bottle with birds in
gilding; Chelsea, gold anchor
period
height 2⅜ in. (6.05 cm.)
Tilley and Co., London

The greatest problem appears to be the connection between the
first and second groups; the modeller may well be the same, but
there is still the difference in the painting to be accounted for. It is
possible that some of the bottles were sent out to independent
decorators, such as William Duesbury or James Giles, (the latter
possessed a flourishing studio in Kentish Town, and worked for
Bow, Chelsea, and other porcelain factories), but the 1754 sale
advertisement announced that the items were "in various beautiful
shapes of an elegant Design, and curiously painted in Enamel",
which seems to indicate that they were already painted before being
sent to the warehouse. The sequence of events suggests that, when
Charles Gouyn split with Sprimont in 1749, he fully intended to
continue making porcelain. After all, he had the secret, and the
demand for porcelain was considerable. We can only suppose that it
was he who invented the "toys", and who, as a jeweller, could mount
them. Then — when he was unable, because of financial difficulties
or bad health, to continue making them — he sold his entire stock
and moulds to Nicholas Sprimont. The latter arranged the sale in
1754, and he had to give himself enough time to sort out the moulds
and perfect his own technique so as to produce his examples in about
1755. He then continued making the bottles until he sold the whole
of the Chelsea factory to William Duesbury of Derby in 1770.
Duesbury carried on until 1784, when he removed the moulds and
entire stock to Derby.

Nicholas Sprimont continued holding sales of his stock right up to the time of his handing over the factory to Duesbury; and, in a sale on the 17th of March 1763, there appeared among other things "a Lady's Toilet with a Looking Glass and Gold instruments, various Shapes of Boxes, and Essence Bottles for ditto of the most rare and truly inimitable Mazarine Blue and Gold, Crimson and Gold . . ." These must have been the late gold-anchor bottles, but the flattened mazarine-blue and crimson-and-gold bottles are of good quality and are rare. (Plate 67.)

Scent bottles were evidently very popular abroad at this time, and Chelsea bottles must have been exported in large numbers. An advertisement that appeared in the *Public Advertiser* of the 3rd of April 1756, and was often repeated, announced:

To be sold by Auction by MR. GELLEY at the Great House, in Great Marlborough-street, The intire Stock of Messrs. Laumas and Rolyat, late of Lisbon, Merchants consisting of 1 hundred double dozen of Chelsea China Knives and Forks silver mounted, several dozen of China Smelling-Bottles mounted in Gold and ornamented with stones of several sorts, as Diamond, Rubies &c.

In 1792, Mr Christie held an interesting sale of "Various Musical Clocks, Pieces of Mechanism, and Other Rich and Valuable Effects, late the Property of Mr James Cox, of Shoe Lane, Jeweller. Which Effects (being now at *Canton* in China, having been sent there at a great Expence of Freight and Insurance) Will be sold by Auction (By Order of the Assignees) on Thursday February 16, 1792 at 12 o'Clock, IN ONE LOT". It is fascinating to think that the rich and varied items listed in the catalogue should have been considered worth exporting to China. Among the articles mentioned are several "rich essence bottles", one of which is priced on the invoice list at £50. Unfortunately for the heirs of James Cox, though the invoice prices amounted to the total of £52,276, the price paid for the whole consignment in one lot amounted to only £12,000.

Lady Charlotte Schreiber and her husband visited Berlin on the 12th of August 1869, and recorded that they "went to Lewy's Dorothean Strasse. Lewy had an exquisite Chelsea smelling bottle but he wanted £8 for it, so with regret I left it". On the 26th of September 1873 they were in Frankfurt, "Busy with the shops, Goldschmidt's, Seligmann's then Backle, Bamberger, and Aultmann; at this last C.S. discovered a small Chelsea flacon, very good, and we heard of a Chelsea bibelot (a gardener carrying flowers), which Aultmann fetched from a private house to show us, and which we eventually bought, though at nearly £5; also we got a Chelsea flacon at Lowenstein's thus adding three to our number of soft paste bibelots. These we consider a great find". When she was in Paris on the 11th of February 1875, she noted that Oppenheim's "had many pretty good things, some of which are put aside for our future inspection; but we at once seized upon and carried away an exquisite Chelsea smelling bottle, formed as a girl smelling at a flower and holding roses, cheap at £7. 12."

Lady Charlotte had a keen eye, as can be seen from her magnificent collection, which she gave to the Victoria and Albert Museum; if she had known what the cost of a Chelsea scent bottle would be a hundred years later, perhaps she would have not hesitated at one for £5.

Other English Porcelain Scent Bottles

Charles Gouyn of the girl-in-a-swing factory, and Nicholas Sprimont of Chelsea, certainly had great successes with their porcelain scent bottles, and it is hardly surprising that few of the other English porcelain factories attempted to compete with them in this field. Naturally, in the 1780s, Duesbury at Derby, who owned all the original Chelsea moulds, was able to produce his versions. Being taken from the same moulds as the gold-anchor Chelsea ones, they are inevitably very close in style, but the later Derby ones are distinguished by their brilliant green-washed bases edged in gilding. In the late eighteenth and early nineteenth centuries, when the influence of Sèvres was at its height, the forms of bottles became less fanciful, and the standard pear-shaped bottles were often painted with flowers or birds, on a rich ground of colour, by painters such as William Dodson. It is interesting to compare bottles made at Chelsea and Derby, particularly the "boy-and-goat" bottles.

The Bow porcelain factory, in London, founded in 1748 and less important only than that of Chelsea, does not appear to have produced many bottles. The one model that seems to have been made there represents Harlequin standing in front of a tree with his hat in one hand and a slapstick in the other. An example of this is in the

PLATE V. (*Enlarged*) "Girl in a Swing" casket enclosing glass scent bottles height 2¾ in. (6.65 cm.) *Winifred Williams Antiques, Eastbourne*

PLATE 68. A scent bottle in white and jasper with blue figures; impressed mark Torner *height 3¾ in. (9.55 cm.) Collection Nina Fletcher Little, Brookline, Mass.*

collection of the late Mrs Meyer Sassoon, while others are reproduced in the catalogues of the Untermeyer Collection and the Emma Budge Collection.

Eighteenth-century Worcester bottles are equally rare; these are interesting in that they take the form of Bristol cut-glass bottles, and bear a marked resemblance to the dated type of glass bottles. The Worcester scent bottles mostly depict oriental subjects, and may possibly have been decorated by the glass-decorators themselves, or by independent painters employed by the factory.

During the nineteenth century, bottles were made in greater numbers, and they reflect the influence of Sèvres rather than of Meissen. Classical shapes became the fashion, and often they had coloured grounds superimposed with panels of landscapes, some

PLATE VI. *(Enlarged)* Hussar scent bottle; Chelsea, "Girl in a Swing" type *height 3½ in. (8.9 cm.) Collection Parfumerie Houbigant, Paris*

77

PLATE 69. A blue jasper bottle
with a portrait of the Prince
of Orange; Wedgwood, 1785
height 2⅓ in. (6.35 cm.)
Collection Nina Fletcher Little,
Brookline, Mass.

PLATE 70. A blue and white
jasper double scent bottle;
Wedgwood
height 3¼ in (8.25 cm.)
Collection Parfumerie Houbigant,
Paris

PLATE 71. A blue jasper bottle with white decoration depicting "A Conquering Hero"; Wedgwood, 1785 height 2½ in. (6.35 cm.) Josiah Wedgwood and Sons, Barlaston, Staffordshire

PLATE 72. A scent bottle in blue and white jasper with Zephyrs; Wedgwood, 1786 height 3½ in. (8.9 cm.) Josiah Wedgwood and Sons, Barlaston, Staffordshire

79

imaginary and others with views of well-known places. Portraits and encrusted flowers took the place of moulded rococo scrolls. The porcelain itself, being technically more perfect, inevitably did not retain the charm of the experimental wares. Bottles made at Derby, Coalport, and the Welsh factories of Swansea and Nantgarw were of a similar nature; the quality of the material and the decoration was good, but in artistic design the eighteenth century *esprit* had been lost.

At Etruria, Josiah Wedgwood succeeded in producing bottles of a classical elegance. Usually in blue and white jasper, they have great quality and achieved a deserved popularity. (Plates 68, 69, 70, 71, 72.)

As Wedgwood made cameos in jasper, which were sent to be mounted at the metal works of Matthew Boulton and Fothergill, it seems probable that he had scent bottles mounted by Boulton too, as at one time Wedgwood was in such close touch with both Boulton and Dr Fothergill, through the Lunar Society, and through discussing with Fothergill the use of foreign clays.

An interesting comment on Wedgwood's techniques is given in the following letter from Josiah Wedgwood to his second son, dated the 16th of April 1788:

> I think I wrote you before that some smelling bottles with Henry IV of France on one side, and his minister Sully on the other, would be very acceptable. The heads are too large I know for this purpose, but they will easily be made less by sinking and taking away part of the shoulder. — The Emperor of Germany on one side and the spread Eagle on the other, — for another sort. This head must be your largest cameo size, the other is quite too large. I shall send you some other heads for these purposes very soon.
>
> Pray let us hear often how my sister Byerley does. All here are well, and unite in kind love to you with
>
> your ever affectionate father
> Jos. Wedgwood

6 'Galanteriewaren', or the Art of Extravagance

THE EIGHTEENTH century may be called the Age of Extravanance, when no gentleman could consider himself one unless he took a gift to his lady-love. During this period he would give his hostess a present in the form of trinkets or (as they became known in Germany) *galanteriewaren*. These included a variety of little objects. One might be a *bonbonnière*, or an *étui* for needles or bodkins, cane handles, and *nécessaires*; or a *carnet de bal*, a patch box, or—probably above all these—a *riekflakon* or scent bottle. On the Continent, especially in Germany and France, porcelain was found particularly suitable for scent bottles, an infinity of extravagant designs being possible, and they were produced by practically every porcelain factory. The models used were quite often the same; the moulds might be taken from one establishment to another by devious means, or copies might be made from finished products. At any rate, since the same proportion of eccentricity found its place in the minds of most rococo craftsmen, it is not surprising that there are so many different types of scent bottles. (Porcelain was not, of course, the only craft strongly influenced by the rococo age; architecture and painting show the same signs, and perhaps even more so does silver.)

About 1750, there can hardly have been a porcelain factory that did not produce its "toys", and it is often a matter of conjecture where the models were first produced. In France they were made at St Cloud, Chantilly, and Mennecy; and, though snuff boxes appear to have been their chief interest, scent bottles were made on occasion. These tended to be of conventional flattened pear-shape, with a diversity of ornamentation, Chantilly choosing

81

chinoiseries in brilliant enamel colours, and St Cloud a more refined style often with figure subjects in gilding; Mennecy produced bottles of more unusual form, such as clog-like shoes, very similar in idea to the *étuis* modelled in the form of a leg that were to be found all over Europe at about this time.

The German porcelain factories appear to have made more scent bottles. The Meissen factory produced a large number, but the models tend to be less original than those of various other smaller German factories. (Plate 73.) It is true that the master of all modellers, Johann Joachim Kaendler, made some of the bottles, and naturally these are very attractive. The Italian Comedy, often taken from Luigi Riccoboni's *Histoire du théâtre italien*, published in 1728, still retained its attraction, and many bottles are in the form of the indomitable Harlequin or one of his fellow comedians; figures of gallants, ladies, and sportsmen were transformed into *riekflakons*, and so were animals. Satire crept in with the figure of a Franciscan friar, who evidently was able to smuggle a lady-friend into his monastery, disguised in a sheaf of corn. (Plate 74.) This subject is engraved from a print known as "Provender for the Monastery", published by John Bowles in about 1760, though an earlier print must exist, as the subject was used by Chelsea as well as Meissen, and probably not later than 1758. Mr Aubrey Toppin, in 1948, discovered this print by John Bowles, and he admits that it is probably a pirated edition of an earlier version. Other Meissen forms included the flattened scroll so characteristic of the rococo age, often painted with entrancing subjects of Italian Comedy scenes, lovers in a landscape, and Watteau-style figures. (Plate 75.) *Chinoiseries* also appeared, and there is a very pretty example of this kind in the Musée Cognac-Jay in Paris; clusters of cherries, plums, and pears, among other fruits, and vegetables were made as well.

The fruit scent bottles have often been ascribed to the Chelsea factory, and, though this attribution is acceptable for a few, more often than not they turn out to have been made at Fürstenberg. This small factory, which was started by Duke Carl of Brunswick in 1747, achieved its best work under the modeller Simon Feilner, who, together with the painter Johannes Zeschinger, was brought from Höchst by Johann Benckgraff. Fürstenberg scent bottles followed such rococo forms as the *putto* and the scrolls with figures from the Italian Comedy figures, or of fashionable gallants and their ladies. Pastoral figures also occur, as well as birds and bottles in the form of wicker-work baskets, usually yellow and with the name of the perfume inscribed on the label (this type was used, moreover, at Meissen

PLATE 73. A gold-mounted bottle;
early Meissen
height 3½ in. (8.9 cm.)
Rijksmuseum, Amsterdam

and Chelsea, and at various minor factories). At Ludwigsburg, from about 1760, similar bottles were produced by the modeller Johann Christian Wilhelm Beyer. His pair of bottles depicting a hunter and a huntress in full dress are particularly delightful. (Plate 76.) Among the other Thuringian manufactures, Kloster-Veilsdorf produced a good series of figures taken from the Commedia dell'Arte, very much in the style of Feilner's Italian Comedy series, and these were adapted for use as scent bottles. (Plate 77.) The boy tussling with a goat at either side of a vine is also found at many of the Thuringian factories as well as at Meissen and Chelsea.

The Fulda factory, founded by the Prince Bishop Heinrich von Bibra, also produced scent bottles, but these are rarely found; again Italian Comedy figures and other standing figures were used, and occasionally these bear the Fulda factory mark of a cross or crowned double F. A curiously grey-looking body was used at the short-lived factory of Kelsterbach; the factory, which suffered many setbacks, flourished only for seven years, under the ownership of the Land-grave Ludwig VIII of Hesse-Darmstadt. Among its extraordinarily detailed and well-finished productions were a number of scent bottles. The modeller Vogelmann was responsible for the vivacious

PLATE 74. A "Provender for the
Monastery" bottle; Meissen
height 3⅛ in. (7.95 cm.)
Collection Parfumerie Houbigant,
Paris

PLATE 75. A Rococo bottle;
Meissen
height 3¾ in. (9.55 cm.)
Collection Claude Leigh, London

PLATE 76. (*Above*) A pair of
porcelain bottles; Ludwigsburg
height 3¼ in. (8.25 cm.)
Collection Parfumerie Houbigant,
Paris

PLATE 77. An Italian comedy
bottle depicting Pantaloon;
Kloster-Veilsdorf
height 3½ in. (8.9 cm.)
Collection Parfumerie Houbigant,
Paris

PLATE 78. A group of porcelain scent bottles; Vienna, Du Paquier, 1718–44
height 2½ in. – 3½ in. (6.35 cm. – 8.9 cm.)
Osterreichisches Museum Für Angewandte Kunst, Vienna

expressions shown on the faces of the figures, which appear to be full
of fun — gallants conversing over a quick *petit verre*, the familiar boy
riding on the back of a goat, and other small figure subjects. A fine
collection of Kelsterbach porcelain still exists at Darmstadt, and the
Blohm Collection also contained a representative number.

Some of the most refined and beautifully decorated bottles, and indeed other forms of *galanteriewaren*, were made at the Vienna factory
during the Du Paquier period between 1719 and 1744. Of silver
and glass shapes, these bottles were often painted with flowers and
chinoiserie figures and had formal borders according to the characteristic fashion of the factory, in black, with the addition of iron-red
and gilding (the so-called *schwarzlot*). Some had moulded decoration
in relief, and were painted in clear fresh enamels with Chinamen;
these scent bottles are as near perfect as any found in the eighteenth
century. (Plate 78.)

Johann Karl Wendelin Anreiter von Zirnfeld, who worked at the
Du Paquier factory, went with his son to the Doccia factory at Florence, where a similar style of decoration was carried out during this
early period, thus giving the Doccia wares a similarity to the Du
Paquier objects. (Plate 79.) I have been unable to trace any Doccia
scent bottles. Some bottles were made at Capo-di-Monte, and these

PLATE 79. A porcelain scent bottle; Vienna, Du Paquier, 1718–44
height 5⅞ in. (14.9 cm.)
Österreichisches Museum Für Angewandte Kunst, Vienna

PLATE 80. A bottle bearing the portrait of Prince Charles Edward and the arms of the Countess of Bristol; Capo-di-Monte *height 4¼ in. (10.8 cm.) Courtesy Sotheby & Co., London*

exist together with cane handles and snuff boxes. Though somewhat grotesque in subject, showing dwarfs and other figures, they possess a certain imaginative quality and a dash of humour; they may well have continued at Buen Retiro when the factory was moved to Spain in 1759. A Capo-di-Monte bottle, which combines fine decoration with mysterious circumstances, has a portrait of Bonnie Prince Charlie on one side, and the coat of arms of Lady Mary Hervey (*née* Lepell) on the reverse. (Plate 80.) In the nineteenth century scent bottles continued to be made as long as the demand lasted, but both size and design of the bottles became debased; these were more suitable for sitting on heavy Empire furniture than for carrying on a chain attached to a ring. Copies of the eighteenth-century models were produced, but even they have a coarseness and gaudiness that would have shamed the early rococo craftsmen.

7 Goldsmiths' & Silversmiths' Bottles

THE WORK of goldsmiths and silversmiths has a longer and richer history than that of any other craft in the world. Both gold and silver were used by the Egyptians, and large quantities of metalwork have been discovered at the site of Troy, the city of Priam, dating probably from not later than 2,000 B.C. Discoveries have also been made of Minoan and Mycenaean metalwork, and also of Greek and Etruscan jewels and plate. Undoubtedly articles intended to enhance human beauty would have been made of gold or silver as well as of glass and terracotta, but little has survived to give any idea of what kind of containers were made for scent.

In England, gold and silver played an important part in the provision of ecclesiastical vessels; and, but for the Reformation, during which many of these were destroyed, we should be able to tell much better what the goldsmiths' work was like. Most of the objects made in gold and silver in the Christian era were meant for use in churches and monasteries. The Church had a large share of the wealth existing at this time, and in fact acted as a benefactor to craftsmen. At the same time there were wealthy noble families, and prosperous merchants, who maintained a high standard in dress and mode of living.

During the Renaissance in Italy, wealth was accompanied by an unsurpassed regard for craftsmanship, and craftsmen combined to produce objects of unrivalled beauty and quality. Foremost among the sixteenth-century Italians was Benvenuto Cellini (1500-77), musician, goldsmith, sculptor, and writer. In his colourful and vain autobiography, he describes the minutest details of his work, which appears to have varied considerably, from medallions and seals for

cardinals, nobles, and the Pope, to settings of rich jewels for Florentine and Roman ladies, and from silver ewers and plate to gold-link
belts and cap-badges. Not only did he tool and chase gold, but he
also taught himself the art of enamelling on gold and silver so that
he could give his jewels enamelled gold settings. Benvenuto also
reveals to us the ways in which the Italian goldsmiths designed
foliage: the Lombards evidently copied the leaves of briony and ivy,
and "the Truscans and the Romans made a better choice, because
they imitate the leaves of the acanthus, commonly called bear's foot,
with its stalks and flowers, curling in divers wavy lines; and into
these arabesques one may excellently well insert the figures of little
birds and different animals by which the good taste of the artist is
displayed". In this manner the earlier technique of carving on ivory
with what are known as "inhabited scrolls" is continued. The same
kind of ornament lasted into the eighteenth and nineteenth centuries,
though the early, freely drawn designs were transformed by baroque
and rococo fashion. Goldsmiths in Renaissance Italy were numerous,
and many are the tales of competition and jealousy that ended at
times in duels or in fights between small bands. The paintings of
the period illustrate the richness of clothes and jewels worn then.
For instance, in the portrait painted by Piero della Francesca of
Battista Sforza, wife of Federigo da Montefeltro, Duke of Urbino,
she wears an elaborately worked gold necklace set with pearls, and
similar jewels are worn in her braided hair. Federigo was an acknowl-
edged patron of the arts, and the jewels worn by his wife bear witness
to the high standard of his craftsmen. Another portrait that depicts
how jewels were made not only to be worn as necklaces or pendants,
but as an intricate enrichment to the clothes, is that painted by
Domenico Ghirlandaio of the Principessa Tornabuoni, the daughter
of a rich Florentine noble. Carpaccio and Titian have left us, in their
paintings, further records of the interest taken in jewels and gold
ornaments by Venetians of the Renaissance.

Perfumes, we know, were then in wide use, and they were im-
ported from the East by way of Constantinople into Venice. Few
bottles of this period survive, but it is probable that the bottles
were made in gold, often with enrichments in enamel.

The output of German metal work during the sixteenth century
was enormous, and followed the same lines as the Italian masters; in
fact, much German work in enamel and gold has been attributed to
Benvenuto Cellini's workshop. The seventeenth century continued
this development. (Plate 81.) Later the main centres were Augsburg
and Nuremberg, both of which became important in the eighteenth

PLATE 81. A carved amber scent
bottle; German, 17th century
height 4 in. (10.15 cm.)
Collection Claude Leigh, London

PLATE 82. A gold and enamel
bottle (one of a pair); by
Johannes Dinglinger
height 2⅝ in. (6.65 cm.)
The Royal Collection at Rosenborg
Castle, Copenhagen

century for their mounts on porcelain boxes and bottles, coffee-pots, and other wares. The best known of the German goldsmiths and enamellers was Johannes Dinglinger, whose monumental gold and enamelled fantasies are to be found in the Grünesgewolbe Museum at Dresden. In these almost theatrical models, oriental figures are carried on elephants and other animals; Eastern potentates are enthroned in pagodas and palaces. Dinglinger's work contains much detail and has great charm, but unfortunately only a few articles can be seen in museums. A pair of scent bottles ascribed to Dinglinger are in the Royal Collection at Rosenborg Castle in Copenhagen, where one can see the perfection in style and application of enamel. (Plate 82.)

Of Russian gold-mounting, some very beautiful examples can be found. (Plate 83.)

In Denmark, silver was widely used, and we can see that the elegant designs of modern Danish silver are inherited, when we compare them with the scent bottles made in about 1680 and engraved with the arms of King Christian and Queen Charlotte Amélie. (Plate 84.)

In England, from the early years of the Tudors, elaborate jewellery was worn, based on the use of gold and enamel with pearls and gems. The styles of dress and the rich brocades and velvets used for these encouraged the wearing of jewellery, and prominent among the necklets and pendants was the pomander. A certain amount of dry perfume or *pot-pourri* was in use, and there exist exquisitely enamelled gold pomanders, pierced and chased. These were worn either from the belt or from a chain round the neck. Silver examples are more often found, in which the compartments are at times engraved with the name of the content, or with a number; shaped spherically, these fall apart into segments, each with its own opening. At this time, pomanders were more in use than liquid perfume.

Such customs of personal adornment continued throughout the Tudor period, when jewellery became more and more lavish, until hardly an inch of material remained on a dress without having a jewel attached to it. The use of pearls became very fashionable; long strings of them were almost down to the ground. During the reign of James I, the splendour of dress and jewellery continued; enamel,

---

PLATE VII. *(Enlarged)* A gold and enamel bottle set with chalcedony panels and the mounts with table- and trap-cut rubies and diamonds; English, late 16th century
height $1\frac{9}{16}$ in. (3.95 cm.) The London Museum, London

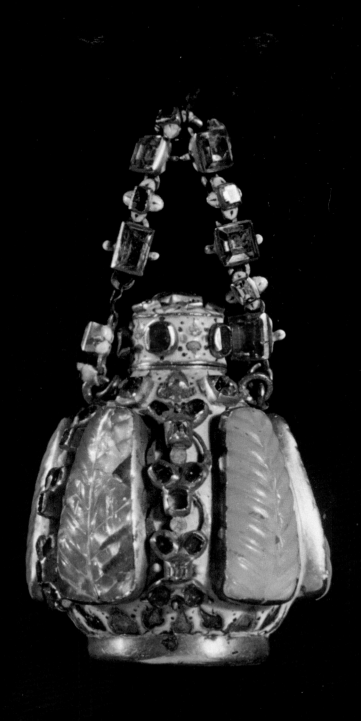

gold, and silver were now mingled in the making of pendants and rings. But from about 1630 dress became more austere, and the only jewels worn were pearls. Though perfumes were used in profusion, these were not often carried on the person, except in a dry form in a silver or gold pomander; and this way of carrying perfume continued until the early eighteenth century. An exception to the rule is a bottle discovered in 1912 buried under a house in Cheapside among other treasures. This find is known as the Cheapside Hoard. (Colour Plate VII.)

The goldsmiths' trade flourished. As early as the reign of Henry VII, an Italian traveller wrote: "In one single street, named Strada, leading to St. Paul's, there are fifty-two goldsmiths' shops, so rich and full of silver vessels, great and small, that in all the shops in Milan, Rome, Venice and Florence put together, I do not think there would be found so many of the magnificence that are to be seen in London". By "Strada", the writer probably meant Cheapside and not the Strand, but he brings out the richness of the trade. Judging from the amount of jewellery worn during the Tudor and Stuart periods, this richness must have been maintained, but it is probable that many of the goldsmiths' shops were destroyed in the Great Fire of London, though some must have survived. Apart from carrying out their craft, goldsmiths also acted as bankers, particularly after the Restoration. Merchants from then onwards preferred to trust the goldsmiths rather than the bankers, and since the goldsmiths' ordinary occupation ceased to a great extent during the years of war and strife, they were only too anxious to take up this profitable concern.

Trade cards and shop-signs of the eighteenth century give a good idea of what kind of trade the goldsmiths carried on. They often combined their trade with that of jeweller, and in this way they were able to produce a large variety of things. (Plate 85.) Few people, I imagine, realize that in the early part of the eighteenth century fountain-pens could be purchased. Among the large number of items announced on the trade card of Richard Boult at the Blue Anchor and Star, opposite Wood Street, Cheapside, are snuff boxes and smelling-bottles, together with stay-hooks, rings, seals, plates, watches, and (surprisingly) fountain-pens. He also stated; "Mourning rings made with the greatest Expedition". Boult was at that address

---

PLATE VIII. *(Enlarged)* Gold and mother-of-pearl *nécessaire* containing glass scent bottles; French, 18th century
height 3¼ in. (8.25 cm.) Collection Parfumerie Houbigant, Paris

PLATE 83. A bloodstone scent bottle with gold mounts; Russian *height 5½ in. (13.95 cm.)* *Collection Parfumerie Houbigant, Paris*

between 1744 and 1753, and he succeeded another member of his family, Michael Boult, who was there in 1713. (Plate 86.)

Another title that many goldsmiths gave themselves is that of "toyman", which, as can be seen from the list of their wares, denotes that they included in their production "toys", which undoubtedly comprised scent bottles and gold *étuis, bonbonnières*, snuff boxes, and other small objects so much in fashionable use. Among the successful

94

PLATE 84. An engraved silver scent bottle with monograms of Christian V and Queen Charlotte Amélie; Danish, circa 1680 *height 3 in. (7.65 cm.) The Royal Collection at Rosenborg Castle, Copenhagen*

PLATE 85. Gold, mocha stone and rose diamonds bottle; English, late 18th century *height 3¾ in. (9.55 cm.) Courtesy Sotheby & Co., London*

95

PLATE 86. *(Opposite)* Trade card, Richard Boult, Goldsmith and Jeweller
The British Museum, London

PLATE 87. Gold scent bottle with a watch and *baisse taille* blue enamel decoration; French, goldsmith Jean Baptiste François Cheret, Paris 1777 *height 4½ in. (11.45 cm.) Collection Parfumerie Houbigant, Paris*

toymen were William and Mary Deard, at the "Star End of Pall Mall, near St. James's Haymarket". They evidently mounted porcelain as well, and sold "Dresden & all other Fine China", besides a "Variety of Fine Toys and all Curiousities in General". Through their trade, the Deards were connected with Horace Walpole, and no doubt they enjoyed the custom of many among the most fashionable people of the court. At times, too, the goldsmiths who were concerned with selling these toys sold also the contents. Joseph Lowe, jeweller at the King's Head near Bartlett's Buildings, Holborn, London, announced that he made and sold "all sorts of Curiousities ... Lavender Honey and Hungary Waters, Fine Snuffs, with curious English and Dutch Toys".

97

PLATE 88. Gold-mounted agate
bottle with gilt decoration;
Louis XV
height 3⅛ in. (7.95 cm.)
Collection Parfumerie Houbigant,
Paris

English gold and silver scent bottles of this period compare very favourably with the French versions in the flow of their elegant rococo waves and scrolls. Sometimes birds or animals were mixed in the design, as in Benvenuto Cellini's sixteenth-century description of Italian goldsmiths' work. But one must remember that Cellini worked for some years at the court of Francis I, and his influence on French goldsmiths' work was strong; the French in their turn were the force behind the export of fashion designs to England in the late seventeenth and throughout the eighteenth century. At this period, enamel was used to enrich decoration, details of flowers and insects or birds often being picked out in coloured enamels to show the intricacy of the design. Various patterns of gold cagework were used, and sometimes encaged bottles, made of a hardstone like jade, agate, jasper, or crystal. They were intricately mounted, with their stoppers usually attached to the neck by means of a small-link chain.

In France, wealth and the enthusiasm of the court for works of art encouraged an enormous output of beautifully made objects, and not the least to benefit from this was the scent bottle. (Plate 87.) Every possible material was tried. It has been said that at the court of Louis XV a different perfume was worn for each day of the year,

PLATE 89. Gold and enamel scent
bottle with enamel bird stopper;
French, Louis XV
height 2¾ in. (6.65 cm.)
Collection Parfumerie Houbigant,
Paris

PLATE 90. *Repoussé* gold bottle;
Louis XV
height 4¼ in. (10.8 cm.)
Collection Parfumerie Houbigant,
Paris

PLATE 91. Gold and enamel bottle and ring; French (Carried by Mme la Princesse Adélaide and later given to the Princesse de Wagram by Louis Philippe on the 13th June, 1848.)
height 4½ in. (11.45 cm.)
Collection Parfumerie Houbigant, Paris

PLATE 92. *(Opposite)* Gold and Japanese lacquer *nécessaire* with two bottles and a funnel; Louis XV
height of bottles 1½ in. (3.8 cm.)
Collection Parfumerie Houbigant, Paris

and so it is likely that at least one bottle a day was used, and probably more, for a belle of the day might have been ashamed to be seen at the opera carrying the same scent bottle on her finger as she had carried the same morning during a walk.

Various techniques were employed for the making of these small but elaborately designed bottles. (Plates 88, 89, 90, 91.) Gold was either beaten out to form scrolls in relief, or chased to form floral garlands or charming *chinoiserie* scenes among the accustomed rococo scroll-work. At times, white and coloured enamels were added to enhance the detail of a bottle. Lazare Duvaux, the *marchand-bijoutier* to Louis XV, showed the popularity of scent bottles in the eighteenth century when he noted in his *Livre-Journal* the items that he sold day by day, and to whom he sold them. On the 6th of August 1750, he sold M. Duflot a gold-mounted flacon in jasper for 168L, and also two étuis in what must have been a type of Vernis Martin, decorated in *le goût des Indes* and containing four flacons; and on the 20th of December 1752 he sold the King "four crystal bottles with different perfumes, 266L", so that he evidently kept a stock of scents in addition to his other wares. There are also several mentions of rock-crystal bottles mounted in enamelled gold, and others of silver in shagreen cases.

Some French scent bottles have beautifully worked cases, of which the most splendid are those in Japanese lacquer. (Plate 92.) These were carved from a larger piece of lacquer and mounted in gold, and they usually contained two or four matching bottles, with a small funnel to fill the bottles. (Plate 93.) Another unusual material for cases containing bottles, or indeed for the bottles themselves, is mother-of-pearl, the medium being particularly well suited to receive applied decoration in gold or silver; the interior in this type of case was generally fitted, as the lacquer boxes were with a bottle in crystal mounted in gold. (Colour Plate VIII.) Of the hardstone caskets, one of the most attractive is in the Musée Cognac-Jay, Paris; it is of green jasper mounted in chiselled gold and containing four bottles. Another there, containing four bottles, is in enamelled gold with a watch set in the lid. A more unusual article, also at that museum, is

a double scent bottle in the form of a double-prowed ship, the centre set with a watch made in a stone commonly called "tiger's eye", of glittering brown, mounted in gold. One of the most delightful bottles is from the Houbigant collection, and is made of crystal mounted in gold in the form of a lantern. (Plate 94.) The faceted sides are enclosed by upright gold columns, and the other mounts are chased with scrolls and colonnades; about a quarter of the way from the top, the lantern opens to reveal a stopper of gold in the form of two billing doves.

Switzerland has been rightly famed for its watches, but it also produced goldsmiths of extraordinary skill. Collectors have always

PLATE 93. *(Opposite)* Lacquered
box containing four glass
bottles and a gold funnel;
French, 1774
height 3¼ in. (8.25 cm.)
Collection Parfumerie Houbigant,
Paris

PLATE 94. Gold and crystal scent
bottle with an inscription
"Amour Fidèle 1768"; French
height 3½ in. (8.9 cm.)
Collection Parfumerie Houbigant,
Paris

tried to acquire Swiss gold boxes, some of which contain mechanized
tricks and ingenious automata. Perhaps the most unusual form chosen
for a scent-container is that of a pistol. (Plate 95.) When the trigger
is pulled, a flower shoots out of the barrel and sprays scent around.
The ingenuity of the design is matched by the richness of the
materials; the gold barrel is chased with flowers and animals, and
the design of the engine-turned gold of the handle shows through
the translucent enamel. As if that were not enough, the handle is
set with pearls. The petals of the flower close and re-enter the barrel
when the cock is re-set. And yet the whole object measures only
4¼ inches.

PLATE 95. Gold and enamel musical scent spray in the form of a flintlock
pistol; Swiss, early 19th century
height 4¼ in. (10.8 cm.) Courtesy Sotheby & Co., London

Another complicated scent bottle is a Swiss one with a gold-and-
enamel musical automaton. (Plate 96.) The gold ground is richly
enamelled and jewelled, and the reverse contains doors, enamelled
on the exterior with figure scenes, which open to reveal the automaton depicting a youth and a girl singing to the accompaniment
of a lady, upon what looks like an exaggerated form of xylophone.
The enamelling was carried out in a Geneva workshop, and the automaton is signed by John Rich, who was working about 1800. One of
the puzzling features is that perfume upsets a watch; we can only
speculate on how long the instrument kept working.

Work in gold and silver maintained its popularity right through
the eighteenth century, and, though the French Revolution tempor-
arily put a stop to the trade, it revived under Napoleon. The custom
of carrying scent bottles continued. However, the heavy classicism
of the Empire style was hardly suited to such essentially frivolous
objects, and they lost much of their charm.

PLATE 96. Gold and enamel automata scent bottle with a watch; Swiss,
enamelled in a Geneva workshop, circa 1800 signed by John Rich
height 8¼ in. (20.6 cm.) Courtesy Sotheby & Co , London

Bibliography

BRYANT, G. E. *The Chelsea Porcelain Toys.* 1925.

Catalogue of the Alfred Trapnell Collection. 1912.

CELLINI, Benvenuto. *Autobiography.* Translated as *Life of Benvenuto Cellini* by A. Macdonnell, 1903. Reprinted 1908.

CHAMBERS, W. and R. *Cyclopedia or An Universal Dictionary of Arts and Sciences.* 1728. Useful for a contemporary view of the subject.

Cheyne Book of Chelsea China and Pottery, The. Edited by Reginald Blunt. 1924.

CHRISTIE'S *Catalogue, 1st–2nd July 1772.*

CHRISTIE'S *Catalogue, 16th–17th December 1772.*

CUNYNGHAME, Henry H. *European Enamels.* 1906.

DE RIS, A. L. T. Clement. *Les Amateurs d'Autrefois.* Paris, 1871.

DIDEROT et d'Alembert. *Encyclopédie.* Paris, 1751–65.

DILLON, Edward. *Glass.* 1907.

DUVAUX, Lazare, Marchand-Bijoutier ordinaire du Roy 1748–1758. *Livre Journal.* Paris, 1873.

GENTILE, Giovanni, and Bertoni. *Encyclopedia Italiana.* 1929–61.

Grande Encyclopédie, La. Par une société de savants et de gens de lettres. Paris, 1885–1901.

HACKENBROCH, Yvonne. *Chelsea and other English Porcelain Pottery and Enamel in the Irwin Untermeyer Collection.* 1957.

HACKENBROCH, Yvonne. *Meissen and other European Porcelain in the Irwin Untermeyer Collection.* 1956.

HAYNES, E. Barrington. *Glass Through the Ages.* 1948.

HEAL, Sir Ambrose. *The London Goldsmiths.* 1935.

HEAL, Sir Ambrose. *London Tradesmen's Cards of the 18th Century.* 1925.

HEAL, Sir Ambrose. *The Signboards of Old London Shops.* 1947.

HIGGINS, R. A. *Catalogue of the Terracottas in the Department of Greek and Roman Antiquities, British Museum.* 1954.

HONEY, W. B. *Guide to Glass in the Victoria and Albert Museum.* 1946.
HONEY, W. B. *Dresden China.* 1934.
HONEY, W. B. *German Porcelain.* 1947.
HONEY, W. B. *Old English Porcelain.* 1928.
HONEY, W. B. *French Porcelain.* 1950.
HUGHES, Bernard. *English Painted Enamels.* 1951.
LANE, Arthur. *English Porcelain Figures of the 18th Century.* 1961.
LANE, Arthur, and Robert Charleston. *English Ceramic Circle Transactions.* Vol. 5, Part 3. 1962.
LAROUSSE. *Grand Dictionnaire Universel du XIX Siécle.* Paris, 1890.
NIGHTINGALE, J. E. *Contributions towards the History of Early English Porcelain.* 1881.
PIESSE, C. H. *Art of Perfumery.* London, 1891.
PRADAL et Malepeyre. *Nouveau Manuel Complet du Parfumeur.* 1895.
RACKHAM, Bernard. *Catalogue of the Schreiber Collection.* 1928.
READ, Herbert. *English Porcelain Circle Transactions.* No. IV. 1932.
ROSSI, F. *Capolavori di Oreficeria Italiana dell' XI al XVIII Secolo.*
SAYER, Robert. *The Ladies Amusement.* 1762.
SCHREIBER, Lady Charlotte. *Journals 1869-1885.* Edited by Montague J. Guest. 1911.
SOTHEBY & Co. *Catalogue of William Edkins's Collection. 1874.*
SOTHEBY & Co. *Catalogue of Otto and Magdalena Blohm Collection. 1960-61.*
WATZDORF, Erna von. *Johann Melchior Dinglinger.* Berlin, 1962.
WEDGWOOD, Josiah, & Sons. *Catalogue of Early Wedgwood Pottery.* 1951.

Index

The figures in **bold type** refer to illustrations.